December, 1981

STOP—THINK—START!

Steps to Change Your Head

and Change Your Life

by

V. Stanford Hampson

Paul & Carolyn —
You are the light
of Love shining eternally

DeVorss & Company
P. O. Box 550
Marina del Rey, California 90291

Your friendship is a
treasure! All good! Stan

Copyright © 1981
V. Stanford Hampson

ISBN: 0-87516-435-8

U. S. Library of Congress Catalog Number: 80-70231

Printed in the United States of America by
Book Graphics, Inc., Marina del Rey, California

This book is dedicated to you, my special friends, who have helped in so many ways along my path from the slopes of Diamond Head to the Enchanted Hill.

Contents

Introduction

We live too much in our own shadows. Surrounded by light we see only darkness. We set out on a bright path of rainbows and then proceed to keep tripping over our own feet. Rightfully, we want to experience more of the wonder of life while we live it.

A friend of mine quipped, "The matter with most of us is plain old 'stinkin' thinkin'." The world is handed to us on a silver platter and we worry about the sterling of the silver. Our cup is filled to overflowing and we grumble that it might have been a better vintage. "Always there is a black spot in our sunshine: it is, as I said, the *Shadow of Ourselves*."[1] Let's stop this kind of thinking and get out of our own shadows.

"What is the hardest task in the world?" asks Emerson. He then answers himself, "To think."[2] Oh, we do it all the time—even in our sleep. However, most of what passes for thinking doesn't do us much good. "To think," in the way that Emerson means, is what this book is all about.

Stop-Think-Start! You can get out of your own shadow and start enjoying more of life's light. Your thoughts can work for you; your dreams can be answered. The

vii

more you appreciate the miracle of your mind, love yourself even as you are, and set about to choose a happier existence, the more fulfilling your life will be.

There are five sections to this book. Each defines a major capacity to enrich your thinking and your life. "To think" begins with a sense of *responsibility* for your own head. Before you seek to make improvements, *accept* yourself as you are. Then you can consciously know what you are doing without destructive game-playing and can successfully execute the *controls* that improve your life. Your thinking defines your life; it also shapes your life. Therefore, what you *envision* determines what you experience. Finally, increased *awareness* of what is, within and without, in silence and joy, opens new horizons of life for you.

Each section is sequential; so is each chapter. Each builds on the previous one and will move you, step by step, out of the shadow of yourself. Then, when you are finished, start all over again. The end of the book brings you back to the beginning—this time with a new consciousness. "To think" is what life is all about. Stop any "think" that is troubling you; think any new "think" you choose. *Stop-Think-Start!*

VSH

PART ONE

Stop—Think—Start!
It's All in Your Head

CHAPTER ONE

Life Can Be Beautiful

You Are Responsible For Your Own Head

It's all in your head! Can you believe it? I hope so, because everything you want in life depends on what's going on in your head. You see, your thoughts produce you. Conversely, you produce your thoughts. Even when you're not aware of what is going on, you are controlling your thoughts. Stop-Think-Start! It's all in your head.

Any kind of improvement occurs through control, and such control begins with responsibility. To improve one of your skills you first accept the responsibility. Then you exert the necessary disciplines to create more and more control of that skill. Responsible thinking is a skill—your most important one. Take responsibility for your own head and then you can start controlling your thoughts as you have never done before.

How does that feel to you? Are you ready to accept full responsibility for your thoughts and your own life? It's a big order. You are more than equal to the task!

Many times we would rather blame our past—distant, or as recently as a moment ago—for what's going on in our lives. Or we confuse responsibility with blame and get

3

angry or depressed because we have no one else to blame for our difficulties but ourselves.

Accept the responsibility for your own thinking. If *your* outlook is up, *you* did it. If *your* attitude is down, *you* did that too. If you are poised, happy, intelligent, loving, enthusiastic and feeling whole and complete within yourself, your own thinking is responsible.

Stop and think about your thinking. Stop any "think" that isn't contributing to what you want out of life. Start any "think" you choose. It's all in your head!

Three baseball umpires were talking in center field. The first one said, "There are strikes and there are balls; I call 'um as I see 'um." The second one said, "There are strikes and there are balls; I call 'um as they are!" The third umpire replied, "There are strikes and there are balls, and they ain't nothin' till I call 'um."

So it is with you! You call the shots of life and they aren't anything until you call them. It's all in your head!

Baba Ram Dass says, "You can't get away from the day because it's all in your head! . . . And the only way to get away is to change your head! Simple as that! You want to change your environment? Change your head!"[1]

Stop! Who does the thinking that gets you upset? Whose thoughts depress and discourage you? Whose thinking makes you worried and tense? There isn't anyone else in your head but you! At other times, who does the thinking that makes you exhilarated? Whose thoughts inspire and encourage you? Whose thinking makes you happy, confident and relaxed? None other than your own. Think! It's all in your head. Events aren't anything "till you call 'um." Win or lose, it's up to you.

Humorist Robert Orben tells about a woman who was addicted to soap operas and listened to them every day. Her husband came home one night and asked "What's new?"

"Well," replied the wife, "Jenny had an abortion; Sam's business went bankrupt; Laura's husband ran away with a belly dancer; little Johnny is in jail for smoking pot; Grandfather Adams' house burned down; Sis won't be able to graduate from high school because she's expecting a baby, and Brother was caught stripping tires from a police car."

"That's incredible!" said her husband. "What's the program called?"

"Life Can Be Beautiful," answered the wife.[2]

Only a soap opera? Not on your life. No matter how incredible it may appear, life can be beautiful, depending on you.

It never has been our problems that define our lives. It never will be. Life has nothing to do with events, but rather with attitudes. What are you thinking about the experiences that you encounter?

Mark Twain said: "Life does not consist mainly, or even largely, of facts and happenings. It consists mainly of the storm of thought that is forever flowing through one's head."

Life consists of the thoughts flowing through your head! When your thoughts are pulling you down, you can stop. You can change your head. You can change your attitudes. Think that life is beautiful and it can be beautiful. It depends on you.

If you're curious about what your attitude is right now, there's a simple test you can take. Earl Nightingale suggests that you simply answer "yes" or "no" to this one question: "Do you think the world is treating you well?"[3] Whether you say "yes" or "no" reflects your attitude toward life. If you feel the world is treating you well, it's because you have that kind of approach to life. If you have a negative attitude, you're going to define the world that way. The real truth of the matter is that life doesn't treat you at all. You have to pay your own way by your thoughts and your own discipline of mind.

Attitude determines everything about our economics, about inflation, about politics, about food supplies, about war, about pollution and everything else. Read what the economists are saying in all the media. Where we go from here is dependent on the attitude of the public. A recession or a depression is a reflection of our own values. Increased national prosperity is also a mirroring of our own attitudes.

How does the world look to you? It looks good if you have that approach to life. Is the world treating you well? It is if you are thinking well. Life can be beautiful.

Sometimes we're slow to believe. We can see how someone else's attitude is complicating his experience but our case is different. When we have a negative situation we think we have to be negative about it.

Certainly, when you have a serious situation you'd better pay attention. Some things will go away if you ignore them but many things won't. However, making yourself unhappy because you have a tough situation won't help at all. Wandering in the maze of your own doubts and fears can actually make matters worse. Instead, you can have a positive attitude in spite of a negative situation. It all depends on you, not on the situation.

Columnist Earl Wilson once told of a fellow who confessed to a friend, "I got married because I was tired of going to the laundromat, eating in restaurants and wearing socks with holes."

"Funny," the friend replied, "I got divorced for the same reason."[4]

It's really all within you. No matter how grim things may be, it's you, yourself, who made them that way. The misery or joy is in you!

Another fellow was the most henpecked husband the psychiatrist had ever seen. This time he had even more troubles. "I have terrible nightmares," the mousey little husband said. "Every night I dream I'm shipwrecked with twelve beautiful women."

"What's so terrible about that?" asked the psychiatrist.

"Have you ever tried cooking for twelve women?"[5]

Think-Start! It's all in your head. Whether your life is a dream or a nightmare, you are defining it so.

We really are funny. We get married and divorced because we look at the same facts in different ways at different times. When we're convinced we love someone, nothing else matters. Likewise, when we convince ourselves we don't like someone, there isn't anything they can do that will please us. Our dreams become nightmares because we have thought them so. It is pathetic—and that is why it is humorous. It is strange, sad and laughable what we do to ourselves.

Even so, the circumstances of your life may not seem funny. You might ask, "How can I laugh when it hurts so much?" Whether you laugh or cry is up to you. That's your reaction. To begin with, whether you name your events a sob-story as dramatic as a soap opera, or a situation comedy, it is up to you. Your life really is funny. It's hilarious how you work yourself up. Remember that time you got angry and did some foolish thing? It's funny now! What you are experiencing today can be funny while you are living it. When you see how you are creating the drama, you are bound to laugh. Life can be beautiful. Set your mind to make it delightfully so!

Sophia Loren was interviewed in the newspaper recently.[6] She is a beautiful, rich, successful person. It was not always so. She and her sister were born out of wedlock, raised by their maternal grandmother in Italy in the most terrible sort of poverty. When filming "Man of La Mancha," she was exchanging childhood memories with co-stars Peter O'Toole and James Coco.

Said O'Toole, "You've no idea how poor I was as a kid. My father was a migratory bookmaker and every few months we had to move from one town to another just to keep ahead of the sheriff. I think I was nine years old before I got my first pair of shoes."

Said Coco, "That's nothing. I'm the son of an Italian immigrant shoemaker. Where I grew up in Harlem, in the Lower Bronx, in New York, my father would take me to the corner candy store once a week for five cents worth of candy. That was the biggest thing in my life."

Replied Sophia in mock amazement to both of them, "You had a father? You had shoes? You ate candy?" She went on to describe the terror of living in Naples during the war as a child, not living—only existing.

You had a father, you had shoes, and you had some candy. How terrible is terrible? How good is good? Each day you make the decision. How's the world treating you? Just how you see the world in your own mind—in your own head. Many people make themselves miserable their whole life long, telling themselves how terrible their childhood was; how awful, unloving, or unforgiving somebody was. Yet was it terrible? It's a dream or it's a nightmare. It's a misery or it's good. It depends on you. The Persian poet sang, "I was upset because I had no shoes until I saw the man who had no feet."

Konrad Adenauer said years ago, "We all live under the same sky, but we don't all have the same horizons."[7] We don't all have the same horizon, and if you don't like yours, Stop-Think-Start! Change your attitude. Get in touch with what's in your head. Stop the counter-productive thoughts; pursue the thoughts that will make your life work.

Life can be piled high with problems and everything can seem to be going wrong. No, you can't put square pegs into round holes. However, you can reshape the pegs, you can reshape your attitude and reshape you. Change your head, and life takes on a new look.

How does life look to you? Are you healthy, happy and prosperous? Are you in pain, misery, feeling unloved and unhappy? How is life treating you? What thoughts are you thinking? Take a responsible look at your own thoughts and you see where the joy and pain are coming from. You call the shots.

A young bride followed her husband to an army camp on the edge of the desert in California. The living conditions were primitive; her husband advised her not to join him, but she wanted to be near him. The only housing they could find was a run-down shack near an Indian village. The heat was unbearable, 115° in the shade; the wind blew constantly, covering everything with dirt.

The days grew long and boring. Her only neighbors were the Indians, who didn't speak any English. When her husband was ordered farther into the desert for maneuvers she was really alone.

The loneliness and the wretched conditions finally got to her. She wrote her mother that she was coming home. Her mother replied with a quick note that included these two lines: "Two men looked out from prison bars; one saw mud, the other, stars." She read these lines over and over again, and decided to start looking for the stars.

The following day she set out to make friends with the Indians. At first, they were not sure of her, but eventually, when they realized she was genuine in her interest, they welcomed her friendship. She studied their weaving, their pottery, their culture and their history—everything she could about them. She studied the desert as well, and it changed from a desolate forbidding place to a thing of beauty. She studied all the different plants and cacti. She collected sea shells that had been left there millions of years ago when the desert had been the ocean floor. Eventually she became an expert on the desert area and wrote a book about it.[8]

What had changed? Her environment was the same. Now she saw it differently. By changing her attitude, she transformed a miserable experience into a thing of beauty and a thing of splendor. Life was beautiful all the time. She changed her head to see it.

In Harry Owens' book, *Sweet Leilani,* he reprints from a Hollywood newspaper an item by Erich Brandeis.[9] The article begins at Sing Sing where a twenty-year-old youth was about to be executed for a rape-slaying. The only visitor that called on him was his mother, who made a special farewell trip, under guard, from the prison where she was serving a thirty-year term for killing her husband. It's not recorded what they discussed in that interview, but just before going to the chair the fellow said to the attending chaplain, "I never had a chance."

"Never had a chance?" questions the author. The article continues, reporting that bandleader Harry Owens made a trip from Hollywood to the Kalaupapa leper colony on Molokai. There he had a long chat with one of the patients, a man who is not only a leper but who is also blind. Harry had come to tell this man that his song "Sunset at Kalaupapa" was one of the hottest things in California, on its way to becoming a smash hit all over the country, and had already earned him five thousand dollars in royalties. The author and composer was Samuel Kuahine.

Never had a chance? Neither of these men had many advantages, but they did very different things with their lives. People who have failed or gotten into unhappy situations often blame life and say they never had a chance. Perhaps it's true they never had a chance to lead a normal life, but they certainly had no worse chance than the blind leper on Molokai, who, in spite of his terrible affliction, could still write about a sunset he couldn't see. One saw mud, the other saw stars. What will it be for you?

I'm convinced life is 90 percent attitude. If that other

10 percent simply won't change, it isn't that significant—because life is mostly attitude. The same facts can be entirely different experiences for different people, depending on the way they look at the experience.

Attitude! It's simple. The way you look at your life is what you experience. Outlook determines outcome.

Remember, facts do not upset you; only your own thinking can do that. In time, you can do something to change your facts—all facts change anyway. Right now there are many things you can do to change your outlook. Start at the beginning. Joyously accept the responsibility for your own head. This is the "start" to think.

Here is an exercise. Read it through; then set the book aside and do it: Close your eyes for a few moments. Breathe easily and deeply seven times. Now tell yourself something like this: "My thoughts are my own. I claim responsibility for my own thoughts. Where I have believed something was disturbing me, I now see my own thinking is all that disturbs me. The way I define situations through my own thoughts makes me happy or unhappy. I am responsible. I am responsible for the way I think. I am responsible for the way I feel. I am responsible." Now smile to yourself. Open your eyes.

Think! It's up to you. It's all in your head. No shoes? No hope? No candy? No way out? As Carlyle wrote, "Every day that is born into the world is like a burst of music, and rings itself all the day through; and thou shall make of it a dance, a dirge, or a life march, as thou wilt."

Only you are in your head. Only you can make you miserable or happy. The desert is still there; the sunset is still there. You shape the peg, you change your head, you change the horizon. "According to your faith it is done unto you."

Go ahead and take that 90 percent control of your life by accepting the responsibility for your own head. Look at yourself. Laugh at yourself! The beginning of all improvement is your own realization that your life depends on what's going on in you. Your outlook sets your outcome. *Start-Think!* Life can be beautiful! It's up to you!

CHAPTER TWO

Misery Is Optional

The Choice Is Yours

Misery is optional. So is happiness. Health is one of your options. So is sickness. All states of mind, body and affairs are really options or choices. You have made a start by accepting the responsibility for your own thinking. The second step of *Stop-Think-Start!* is to start controlling your life through your mind by exercising your various options.

I was once the guest speaker for a meeting of a group of people seriously trying to work with and solve their problems. They are called Al-Anon, a group of persons who have in common the fact that someone in each of their lives is afflicted with an alcohol problem.

It was a good meeting. I haven't the slightest idea what I spoke to them about, but I do recall vividly what one woman there shared with me. She told me she kept a book of the ideas that helped her the most. She wrote them down as they were received so she could review them—which she did frequently. The first entry was, "Misery is optional." It's an exciting concept and capsulizes this next step of *Stop-Think-Start*.

Too often we equate suffering with problems; we think

of them as one and the same. There is a big difference. You can have numerous difficult situations—problems galore—and not be miserable. I've known some people who had no problems and were still unhappy. Start to think! What is happening to you does not define your state of mind, although your state of mind does define what is happening! Life can be beautiful if you choose it that way.

The Buddha said, "Suffering is ignorance." That's it! Since life is all in your own head, unhappiness of any kind must be from your own foolishness. Remember, you have already accepted that responsibility; now, see your responsibility as one of choices. Any misery or suffering is a choice in one of two ways; once you recognize them, the suffering dissolves.

First of all, suffering is ignorance of the difference between events and reactions. You can be sick, poor, rejected, and "the show can still go on." It is always your choice to be unhappy or happy regardless of events. Your response is your option. You choose how you will feel and what you will do. By recognizing that misery is optional you have separated the event from your reaction. Something happens; put a stop there! Stop! Put a space between what is happening and what you are doing with it. You have immediately shifted gears to a new level of understanding and are preparing for a higher level of living.

Let's suppose your marriage is falling apart. It's happened in many people's lives, and it's a serious experience. You could choose to react in many ways—be unhappy, strike out at someone in anger, withdraw into a shell of depression, even tell yourself it's the end of the world. Instead, separate the pending divorce from your reaction.

Stop! Put a space between what is happening and how you are going to react. *Start-Think!* with a stop. Whatever you do is your choice.

Robert Louis Stevenson was seriously ill while writing many of his most delightful verses. He would work as long as he could, sometimes for only minutes at a time. He said he refused to let the medicine bottles on his mantle determine his life. He had exercised his option to react by his own choice. So can you.

You frequently hear comments such as: "She ruined my day;" "You make me so mad;" "These kids are driving me crazy." What you want to hear inside yourself is the reminder that such reactions are options. Some event has taken place. It has nothing to do with the option. Misery is optional—a clear choice. Unrewarding choices are made in ignorance; you can stop. It's all in your head.

You never *need* to suffer. That is an exciting realization to dawn in your awareness. The longest you ever need to be miserable is about thirty seconds. That's right: *thirty seconds!* That is long enough for you to recognize that misery is an option you don't have to choose. You can choose to pray, to count stars in the sky, to do some physical activity, to get busy solving the situation. Without grief or self-pity, you can opt to measure your powers rather than your problems. You never need to be ignorant again; you can stop confusing situations with your responses.

Secondly, suffering is ignorance of the fact that the laws of the universe are always consequential, not accidental. You can have miserable situations because you have set those laws into motion without knowing the consequences. That's ignorance.

The intelligence that holds the universe together and makes it an ever-renewing, always-creating activity functions logically. We are not punished *for* our mistakes. We are punished *by* our mistakes; we receive the natural consequences of our actions. We really punish ourselves.

An illness, for example, may have its cause in something you thought or said yesterday; it may be from an activity in your head a long time ago. It could be from something you ate. It could be due to a pattern of believing or living. It could be simply a virus that is going around. (You don't have to catch it, but you can, before you stop the old thoughts and life patterns and think in a better way.) An illness could have any and all of these causes at the same time. You wouldn't have created the causes if you knew better. The causes are so complex you may never discover them all. It's still ignorance.

If you accidently eat something that isn't good for you, your body will probably react in a way to heal itself. (Remember, you don't have to be miserable just because your body is.) However, the point here is that ignorance of what you were doing caused the misery.

Universal law is generally consequential in a specific way. That is, ignorance of health will not affect your prosperity. Likewise, knowledge of health will not benefit your finances. You might wish you could do a good deed today and thereby earn "points" against the challenges of tomorrow. Life doesn't work that way. Knowing how to make money doesn't help you understand your family. You need to learn about that separately. Being a good sport won't necessarily do anything for your health. Health is something else to learn.

Someone handed these lines to me one day. I prize

them, even though I don't know where they came from. They are titled, "Epitaph on a Tombstone in Oklahoma:"

> Here lies Jake Dwiner
> Who was killed by a circular saw.
> He was a good citizen,
> An upright man,
> An ardent patriot,
> But of limited information
> Regarding circular saws.

Obviously, being a good person is not enough. The ancient Greek philosophers talked about virtue being worthy for its own sake. Virtue is great, but it won't help you much with circular saws. Only knowing what you're doing will. You might be the most generous and kind person in the neighborhood; however, if you step off your roof the logical consequences will still be abrupt. Emerson wrote, " . . . learn that everything in nature, even dust and feathers, goes by law and not by luck . . . and that what he sows he reaps."[1]

Misery is optional—the result of ignorance. Events are not reactions. When you separate the two, you never need to suffer again. Misery is the result of choices that create miserable conditions. When you suffer it's because you've chosen to do so out of ignorance. Don't suffer, solve! Define your life by your powers, not by your problems. Choose to think, say, and do the things that get you what you want out of life. When things don't turn out the way you intended, choose to separate those results from your reactions; don't choose to be unhappy in any event.

If you need to solve something, do it. If you have a problem in any area of your life, you simply haven't built the answer to that problem into yourself yet. Don't waste any more time. *Start-Think!* It is in your head!

Misery is ignorance; joy is knowledge. You can build the answers you need regardless of events. Do it! You can set better laws into motion. It's up to you. Don't be miserable again, at least for any longer than thirty seconds—just long enough to put a mental space between events and what you do with them. You are separate from things. Your medicine bottles or unpaid bills or anything else do not cause you unhappiness. Nobody ruins your day but you. You do it to yourself. There's nobody out there punishing you. You're getting the results you set into motion.

Now you know. You can't be ignorant again; you can't be miserable again. If you need to learn about health, prosperity, joy, or circular saws, do it. The following chapters in this book will give you specific techniques to do just that. At this point, decide to exert your own control over your own head.

Here is an exercise that will help you to practice controlling your options. Imagine a large "wedge-of-silence" in your mind. Put this wedge between yourself and any reaction. The sharp point can penetrate any state of mind. Without force, drop it in. As it settles it widens. The silence fills your mind. Think about some specific event; insert this wedge between the event and yourself. Practice "seeing" this wedge-of-silence widen and fill your consciousness.

You are delaying your responses. At first you may only delay them momentarily. That is a good start! Life can be beautiful; you have claimed the responsibility to make it so. Now you are building a new control into your consciousness. You are beginning to think—truly! Upon recognizing an event, immediately place a wedge of silence in your mind. You do not need to suffer. It is all in your own head.

Ella Wheeler Wilcox sings these lines to spur you on:

> With every rising of the sun,
> Think of your life as just begun,
> The past has cancelled and buried deep
> All yesterdays: there let them sleep.
> Concern yourself with but today;
> Grasp it and teach it to obey
> Your will and plan,
> Since time began, today has been
> The friend of man.
> You and today: a soul sublime
> And the great heritage of time.
> With God himself to bed the twain,
> Go forth, brave heart; attain! Attain![2]

Misery is optional. You choose to be miserable and you choose miserable situations. You do so only in those areas in which you are ignorant. *Stop-Think-Start!* Since the responsibility for your own head is yours, you can make responsible, intelligent choices. What is happening to you does not define your state of mind; your state of mind defines what is happening. Life can be beautiful. Choose it that way.

CHAPTER THREE

Why Do Things Get in a Muddle?

Think: STOP!

Our lives are complicated. That's a fact. But, it's all in our heads, remember? We ourselves make it that way. Just look at our procedure for drinking tea! We boil the water to make it hot and then add ice to make it cold. We put in lemon to make it tart and add sugar to make it sweet. Then we try not to drink it because of the caffeine.

Some people take pills to speed up and then more to slow down. Many people today take the drug "alcohol" to relax and take aspirin for the consequent headaches. I know a man who washes down his tranquilizers with hot, black coffee. He cannot seem to figure out why they don't work for him. One cure often cancels another, and many cures lead to more complicated conditions. Norman Shealy, M.D., has on the wall of his waiting room, "So we wind up with the pill that relieves the anxiety brought about by the fear that our tranquilizer may not counteract the stimulant used to offset the depressant." Why do things get in such a muddle?

21

Some days, nothing seems to go right. The people who populate your personal world have plans of their own—often vastly different from what you think they should be. Your daughter's bedroom is a mess, and your son won't get a haircut. The dog just chewed a couch pillow—foam rubber is all over the living room. The weeds are winning their war on your garden. The more things you accomplish on your daily agenda, the more things seem yet-to-be-done. Yes, things do get complicated and muddled!

Your third step to really think is to think about stopping. Who creates the time-schedules and the time-demands? You do. Instead of spreading your energies in so wide an arc that you feel harried, tense, and running-scared, *think less of more and work more on less.* Choose to let go of many of the things you now think are so important and try to control fewer events. Raise the threshold of your concerns. *Start-Think!*ing a STOP!

Gregory Bateson wrote a marvelous metalogue called, "Why Do Things Get in a Muddle?"[1] The conversation goes back and forth trying to define what are "things," when are they muddled, and what is tidy or neat. My wife's definition of neatness regarding my private work areas is far different from mine. Likewise, her orderliness often defies me. One person's "tidy" is another's muddle.

I have a picture over my fireplace. I like it centered there. If it were moved over a foot or so it would be off balance and "muddled." It needs to go in the center. At least, I think it does. Well, one inch either way probably wouldn't matter. So there are at best very few places it looks tidy to me. I define what is orderly and what is not orderly. You may see the whole thing differently. Is it any wonder we can have disagreements when it's all in our own heads!

You could spell the word "LIVE" out of large wooden letters, and place them on a table.[2] Shake the table repeatedly; the letters won't spell anything. The chances are a million to one they won't even spell "EVIL" which is "LIVE" backwards. We define what words in our language we can spell with those letters, and random placement would not likely conform to the very few places we would define as logical or "tidy."

The same phenomenon occurs whether we are considering a skill, creating a thing of beauty, defining living standards, or plain thinking. Things get in a muddle precisely because there are so many more ways to define muddle than order. An appropriate thesis could be: "All things go toward muddle." That is, all the universe tends to move toward variety and change. The more ways you and I limit what we call "tidy," the more we increase our odds of muddle. It IS in our heads! We DO create our own frustrations and make our lives complicated and difficult.

Marcus Aurelius said, "The universe is change: our life is what our thoughts make it."[3] We set in our own heads the limits that trouble us. By our "holding on to tidy" and trying to "stop it all from happening" we find muddle. In fact, we create it.

If you want to keep things orderly but have defined only a few ways order can be established, things will always be in a muddle. If you plan other people's lives to conform to your expectations of how they should be and live, you'll find those people in a muddle. You define the threshold above which you will feel confused. Play the odds! You're defeating yourself before you ever get started.

You are the problem. You are doing it to yourself. Life can be beautiful if you'll think: STOP! See that the world around you is change. Stop setting yourself up to feel muddled. Goethe wrote, "Man seeks his inward unity, but his real progress on the path depends upon his capacity to refrain from distorting reality in accordance with his desires." Ride the horse the way it's going! Stop trying to make everything and everyone fit your plans. All things move away from your set limits for one simple reason: there are so many other ways they can be.

Adler speaks of people who " . . . attempt to pigeon-hole every activity and every event according to some principle which they have assumed valid for every situation . . . We have the impression that they feel themselves so insecure that they must squeeze all of life and living into a few rules and formulae, lest they become too frightened of it. Faced with a situation for which they have no rule or formulae, they can only run away."[4]

You don't have to be one of those people. Let it go. Think-Stop!

Right now, raise the threshold of your concerns. In two basic ways stop letting so many things disturb you. First of all, *think less of more*. Secondly, *work more on less*.

To think less of more, let go of some of the pigeon-holes you live by. All those demands are in you. All those exacting standards of neatness are yours alone.

Let them go. Start by listing all the things that are essential to your happiness. Write down the things and conditions you couldn't live without. You'll find that most of them are not really necessary at all. The O'Neills suggest completing the sentences "I need . . ." and "I want . . ."[5] Write them all down. Look closely and you'll see that you could survive without most of them.

Alan Lakein tells his clients to write out all their responsibilities in three categories: A. Top priority; C. Low priority; and B. Those things in the middle you can't quite decide. Then put *B* and *C* lists away; work only on those items in *A*. Now you have narrowed your concerns to those that are most significant.[6]

Several persons have suggested a question to bring your life into focus. Ask yourself, "What would I do if I knew I had only one week to live?" It can be an effective way to redefine your responsibilities. You have certain things to attain that are significant. Most of the things that occupy your time and energies are not important. When your concerns are numerous, so are your chances of confusion. Think less of more; stop making demands that so much of life follow your personal plans.

Think-STOP! Force yourself if necessary. Think less of the many things you once thought important. So little is really enough.

In Alexander Solzhenitsyn's novel, *One Day in the Life of Ivan Denisovich,* the heroic-tragic Ivan goes to bed at the end of the day fully content. He is politically exiled to Siberia where the conditions and the cold are below the levels of mere existence. Yet he is content: "He'd had many strokes of luck that day: they hadn't put him in the cells; they hadn't sent his squad to the settlement; he'd swiped a bowl of kasha at dinner . . . and he hadn't fallen ill . . . Almost a happy day.''[7]

So little is enough. Life can be beautiful in the most miserable of situations. Let go of the non-essentials. Think less of more.

The second way to raise the threshold of your concerns is to work more on less. Try to control fewer events. Look at your life and in the famous words of Thoreau: "Simplify, simplify . . ." Schedule your day so there is room for the unexpected. Only you set yourself up to try to accomplish so much that you are overwhelmed by what you have to do. Rather than have landscaping that requires all your energies, plant your yard so you don't have to be fighting it all the time. Keep it simple.

Obviously, your daughter's sense of "tidy" is different from your own. You could make both your lives easier by staying out of her room and only imposing your sense of order on mutual living areas. If your son's hair gets down to his knees, it won't affect *your* health and well-being. Let go! Think: STOP!

Who knows, you might even learn to drink your tea straight, without all the complications. You may even opt for plain water! Furnish your home and work areas so you don't always have to fight for order. You cause yourself to be tense about your children or your guests if you have created a home that defies relaxation. A friend of mine says, "If you can't afford to easily replace anything in your home, don't have it." That might be extreme, but his principle is right. Why create situations where you can't enjoy your guests? Simplify your life so you are not so much trouble to yourself. Work more on less. It's all in your head.

You are being neurotic when you set up complications in life and become unhappy. You create the confusion to begin with. It is very important to see that. Life isn't fighting you—you are fighting life. Your thinking has created the confusion; your thinking can straighten it out.

"Suffering is always the effect of wrong thought in some direction," says James Allen in his book, *As A Man Thinketh*. "It is an indication that the individual is out of harmony with himself . . . A man only begins to be a man when he ceases to whine and revile and commences to search for the hidden justice which regulates his life. As a man adapts himself to that hidden justice, he ceases to accuse others as the cause of his condition, and builds himself up in strong and noble thoughts. He ceases to kick against circumstances, but begins to use them as aids to his rapid progress."[8]

The nature of the universe is variety. So don't try to make so many things go your own way. Emerson said, "Do what you can, summer will have its flies." Decide what is truly important and simplify your life. Think less of more and work more on less.

Whenever you feel that the world is against you, stop. It is time to simplify. Take one whole minute to sit down and think: STOP! One minute is all you need to stop the muddle in yourself. There are many techniques we will consider later; for now, work on the importance of a simple STOP. Remind yourself of your own *responsibility* for your own head. Place a wedge-of-silence that widens as it settles in your mind. *Decide* to simplify the scope of things you try to control and focus on fewer concerns. Think less of more and work more on less. *Start-Think!* and Think-*Stop!*

Rather than creating more pigeonholes and stricter definitions, let it all go. Let go of the limits you have set on some person. Stop thinking life should fulfill your particular definition of order. Your suffering is in your own mind. To change the muddle, change your mind. Get in harmony with yourself.

Life can be beautiful. Your outlook shapes your outcome. Take responsibility for your own head. Any misery is optional. So are joy, health, and plenty. Be responsible enough to make intelligent choices. If things seem muddled, you know where that is coming from. Think less of more and work more on less. Simplify, simplify, simplify! Think: Stop!

PART TWO

Stop—Think—Start!
Become Grounded in Yourself

CHAPTER FOUR

Look Before You Leap

Know Where You Are Before You Go

If you don't know where you are, how can you get anywhere else? You have to start in the place where you are. So where is your head? Your whole head? This requires a real analysis, a confrontation, a facing of your thoughts and feelings.

When you take responsibility for your own head, frequently you will try prematurely to do something to improve the situation. Then you are fragmented. Your thoughts are going in one direction, your feelings are wandering in several more, and your potential is being wasted. There is an intermediary step between responsibility and action.

Look within yourself and embrace everything you find there. The joy and the hurt, the expanse and the grief, the openness and the loneliness, or whatever you are experiencing must be recognized. Wherever you want to go, you have to take your whole self with you. When all energies are working together for the same objective, you will accomplish much more. After recognizing responsibility, accept where your head is now. Don't try to do

31

anything about it now, just see what is there. Don't be afraid, you can face anything! In fact, before you can go forward you must be sure of your current ground.

To use a map, you need two points of reference—first, where you want to go and second, where you are now. Without either point of reference, you are essentially lost. Once a traveler who was lost stopped a man beside the road to seek directions. The man told him to go so-many-miles in one direction and then in another, then stopped and decided that wasn't right after all. Then he began to give a new set of directions and also cancelled them. After several tries he concluded, "Well, I guess you can't get there from here."

Actually, you can go anywhere from anyplace. The only "here" that you cannot go from is an unknown "here." If you don't know where you are, then you can't get anywhere. *Stop-Think-Start!* Explore where you are before you seek a new direction.

It is an old adage, "Look before you leap!" Look where you're going before you take off. In another way this old saw is also true. Look at where you are before you go anywhere. Look at your "here" before you leap for a "there." Such inner observation integrates your consciousness. Look at your thinking-feeling process and learn where you are.

This is not to say you must analyze your every move. Sometimes it will not be necessary. You will go from one area of awareness directly to another. You choose not-to-think in a certain direction and it works. With Scarlett O'Hara, you "won't think about that today." When done as a deliberate action, and not out of fear, it is an effective way to avoid unhappiness. To really be effective it is usually coupled with affirmation. That is, since the mind cannot maintain a vacuum, you must then think about something creative to replace the unwanted direction. Rather than thinking about your problems, you can decide not to think about them. Then you go one step further and decide what you will think about instead. It's your head, so you can think about anything you want to. However, such direct shifting of awareness is not always possible. You will know. The tendency is to rush while the greater need is to stop.

You see, when the error itself is conceptual, when the problem is really the way in which you look at things, then you can't get your mind off the way the mind looks. It's not what you're looking at, it's what you're looking with. When the "evil" is conceptual, you can solve it only by seeing it with a new concept.

Sometimes, I can say "I'm not going to look there; I'm going to look here," and it will work. I don't want to think in terms of the problem, I want to think in terms of the possibility. I lift my vision to that which is positive, and it works. However, there are other times it's not a matter of a problem or a possibility. It's a matter of what I'm thinking through. Therefore, no matter where I shift my awareness, nor how hard I try to pray and think positively, I'm simply not getting anywhere. The problem is all in my head. The problem's still up here, in the perception, in the core of belief, in my basic belief system. The way around such a block is to look more closely at where I am. I must observe my thoughts and feelings.

If you attempt to change consciousness and are filled with fear, then you are running scared to noplace. If you are avoiding people, events, or thoughts and feelings because you are afraid of them, you have given them more power. Where there is fear, there is power. At such times, even your prayer-work becomes a type of avoidance and doesn't help you much at all. Avoidance doesn't solve anything because the very act of avoidance is keeping alive the thing to be avoided. When based on fear, avoidance is actually an affirmation that there is something to be afraid of.

Dan Greenberg has started working on a book entitled, *How To Make Yourself Miserable*. One morning when he was working on the book he looked at his watch and realized that the dial and the numbers were radium. He began to worry about having that much radium next to his body, so he went to his neighborhood jeweler on a fast run and asked him to take the radium off his watch. The jeweler said he would, but wanted to know why.

"Well," said Dan, "it's very simple. I just don't think it's safe to have radium so near my body. Look at what happened to Marie Curie."

The jeweler said, "That is completely ridiculous. The two stone lions on the front of the New York Public Library have a lot more radium than your watch."

Did that ease his fears? No, he said, he just never went back to the library.

Where are the stone lions in your life that you avoid? Are there things you are not facing? Some things that worry you can be handled by ignoring them. Other things cannot be handled by even the most creative avoidance. Given time, they only get worse. At such times, a bigger-than-usual stop is necessary. Look more closely before you leap.

Naturally, some things are better avoided. You can

prevent addiction by simply avoiding addictive substances. You avoid many accidents with caution. You avoid bankruptcy by being able to pay your bills on time. Even some personal fears cause no problem. If you are afraid of heights, you can avoid climbing ladders without too much inconvenience. If you are afraid to be alone, you can fill your life with people and that can be perfectly all right. Only when an avoidance becomes an uncomfortable handicap is it necessary to do anything about it. If your life isn't working you need to look in your head!

Be conscious of what you are doing. When your life is motivated by unconscious needs, you are "playing games" with yourself and everyone else. Deceptiveness is destructive. If you are avoiding something, admit it to yourself. If you can avoid the stone lions without much disruption, let it go. There are many other things to do. If and when your avoidance becomes hazardous, take steps to know where you are and where you want to go. The key here is to be sure you are knowing what you are doing!

Our lives can be filled with avoidance of the nature that Greenberg jokingly tells on himself. We are half-asleep and spending our energies unconsciously avoiding much of life. We observe and hear things around us but fail to bring them into full awareness. Our minds play a game with us called "Let's pretend it isn't there." We think that if we were to admit to ourselves what is happening and how we're feeling about it, we might be angry—and that is a feeling "nice" people are not supposed to experience. We might have to make a decision. We might not know how to react. So we play "Let's pretend" he isn't obnoxious, and I'm not upset, and this situation isn't happening. Then when things get intolerable, we act surprised. "Suddenly" the marriage disintegrates, the boss lowers the boom, or our finances are disastrous. We assure ourselves, and anyone else who will listen, that there was no clue. That's ridiculous. We must have known that the marriage is in trouble. We must have known the money isn't coming in. There have been signs all along the way, and we have avoided looking at them.

The conscious deliberate action of avoidance is an important technique. I call it "denial." This is the act of consciously withdrawing power from a given state of mind. Some people think denial is "playing like something undesired isn't there"—burying your head in the sand. That's being an ostrich—which not only hides its head but presents a most tempting target! That's the unconscious game of "Let's pretend" again.

Denial is seeing the facts and recognizing that they do not need to remain as they are. No set of facts is permanent. All things can change. A great freeing activity of awareness is to see that you are not bound by a certain set of circumstances. You can change. Events can change. But you have to look to see it! There is nothing to be afraid of when you look!

I heard a clever phrase, attributed to Bernie Gunther, "Turn your avoidance into a void dance." Change an avoidance by facing it. Fear faced dissolves—it is a festering void. Once you see it, there is nothing there. See it as it really is—all in your own head! Look in your head to see where you are. Look before you leap. Turn your avoidance into a void dance!

Here is an important paradox. Denial is both an

avoidance and a confrontation. When you consciously avoid something, and can do as you wish by completely ignoring that something, you are denying it. However, before you can deny "it" you should know what "it" is. There is a brief step in there that is often overlooked and can be most significant. Look at what it is you would change. Face it; confront it. All illusion can be stopped by seeing that it is an illusion. It's all in your head, remember! So *Stop!*

Stop-Think! Stop merely thinking, to think about your thinking. In fact, an important way to stop a trend of thought is to look at the thoughts themselves. This action is in itself a shift to a higher abstraction. Thinking about thinking is a higher logic than thinking. Talking about talking is a higher level of abstraction than talking. On a deeper level of logic, you encounter thoughts you wish to affirm and others you want to deny or constrict. Denying negation is a great negation in itself. It doesn't need to be constricted. Just see it for what it is.

To think is one thing; to think about thinking is something else. When you are fighting the dragons of life they seem very real. When you are looking at your thoughts about the dragons they take on a different perspective. Effective confrontation is simply looking at your way of looking at things.

You will remember when Alice and the Queen were playing croquet in Wonderland. The Queen repeatedly decreeed of Alice, "Off with her head!"

" 'Nonsense!' said Alice, very loudly and decidedly, and the Queen was silent.''[1]

Alice had looked at the situation carefully and realized, "Why, they're nothing but a pack of cards, after all.

I needn't be afraid of them.'' She looked at her fears and saw them for nothing. Then they were finished.

Like Alice, when you look at the situation causing you concern, you often find by confrontation a whole new freedom. If you cut your finger, you would not only rush for a band-aid. You would cleanse the wound first before you attempted to protect it. Your attempts to solve situations are sometimes "band-aid therapy" applied over a dirty wound. Then progress is slow. Cleanse the wound properly and then apply the band-aids to aid the healing. Perhaps, when you look, you will see that you don't need a band-aid. The healing has already taken place.

This might sound negative, but it's not. It's following responsibility for your own life with an acceptance of what you find. You must be able to say, "This is MY problem." Until you get down to that point you're playing avoidance.

Too much identification with a problem would, naturally, give it more power. You don't want your everyday conversation to be "my headache" and "my problem" and "my miserable marriage." That would be constantly tying these things to yourself.

An excess of identification would be unhelpful. But don't let that fact justify an absence. No identification with problems is also unhelpful. Face a problem to solve it.

Dr. Herbert Benoit says it this way: ". . . We can prove directly, intuitively, the illusionary character of anguish. If in fact at a moment at which I suffer . . . I shift my attention from my thinking to my feeling, if, leaving aside all my mental images, I apply myself to perceiving in myself the famous moral suffering in order to savor it and to find out at last what it is—I do not succeed . . . of suffering itself I do not find a scrap. The more I pay attention to the act of feeling, withdrawing thereby my attention from my imaginative film, the less I feel. And I prove then the unreality of anguish.''[2] Fear faced dissolves. Look at it!

Let us suppose a famous man walks up to you. Your conditioned reaction is to feel inferior, inadequate, and unhappy. So before those feelings start—at least as soon as they do—just look at them. As you look at your feelings you are no longer producing the same emotions and you will feel differently. By observing your feelings, you may not have the feelings at all. At least, you have started on a path of being grounded that will eventually lead to freedom. When you look at your thoughts and feelings to observe what they are doing, you have embraced a new consciousness. The anguish, if not gone completely, will certainly be diminished. *Stop-Think!* to *Start-Think! Stop! Look* before you do anything else!

Fritz Perls said, ''Without a center, everything goes on in the periphery and there is no place from which to work, from which to cope with the world . . . This achieving the center, being grounded in one's self, is about the highest state a human being can achieve.''[3]

You can be grounded in peace. Look at your thoughts and feelings. Look and see the void you have made out to be ''something'' and have been avoiding. Turn your avoidance into a void dance: (1) Sit quietly and give your attention to your breathing. (2) Look at something that has been causing you concern. Look beyond the ''trouble'' itself to your troubled thoughts and feelings.

(3) Give a human shape to the fear, worry, anger—whatever you see. See this thought-emotion as a separate part of yourself. (4) Mentally take hands with this part-of-yourself and imagine that the two of you are standing, and then begin to dance. Move rhythmically into a waltz, polka, tango, square-dance, or something you make up. Most probably you will begin with something slow and quiet and then maybe try all sorts of dances together. Occasionally, try to catch the "eye" of your partner. Move together harmoniously. (5) Now become quiet in yourself. Breathe deeply. (6) Now ask yourself: Do those negative thought-feelings seem different now?

As you shift awareness from outer things to interior responses, you see only specters where you once were seeing monsters. As you look at these inner ghosts they dissolve before your eyes. You were frightened by nothing! You were running from a shadow!

When you know this you don't need to run any more; you don't need to pretend. You don't have to avoid the stone lions at the entrance to the New York Public Library, or anything else. You know where you are. You're in touch with yourself and consequently you can be centered. Only emotions to which you consistently give energy will sustain themselves. So look at them—you're not giving them energy by only looking at them. You're looking; you're thinking about thinking, not just thinking. Know where you are before you go on. *Stop-Think!* to *Start-Think!* Look before you leap!

CHAPTER FIVE

Beyond Your Hat and Your Boots

Practice Loving More of Yourself

I believe with Walt Whitman that a man's not all included between his hat and his boots. Each of us is more than he appears to be. We are many persons inside our skins, many facets and dimensions. Some of the various sides of our nature we recognize. Some we would probably like to eliminate. Many we have never even acknowledged. Beyond what we know of ourselves—beyond our hat and our boots—lies an undiscovered mosaic of multiple parts. We are many personalities rolled into one.

Your strength lies in affirming your multiple selves—your subpersonalities. Otherwise your life is experienced as fragmented parts, moods are extreme, meditation doesn't give any peace, and prayer doesn't seem to do any good. When you embrace your entire being, you harness all your energies to go in whatever direction you eventually choose. You have the authority within yourself to regulate your life. Rather than feeling dismayed about your multiphasic personality, you can delight in all its

41

glory. The gentle touch of love, generously bestowed upon yourself, enables you to be and do all that you seek in life. Start now to discover and enjoy that which lies beyond your hat and your boots.

Polonius gave seemingly wise counsel to his son, "To thine own self be true, and it must follow as the night the day, Thou canst not then be false to any man."[1] The ancient Greek advice is similar: "Know thyself." It might appear that there is only one "self" with which to become acquainted and be true. Have you ever wondered, "Which self?" When part of me wants to run, another screams, while yet another wants to stand his ground, which "self" should I know and follow?

The bible speaks of creating man in "our" image and making him "male and female." Every language has its limitations, and translators often cloud issues rather than clarifying them. However, Genesis could certainly be referring to more than one phase of a person. We are each one male and female in many ways—we combine all the stylized characteristics of each. We are leader and follower; aggressive and passive; firm and tender; stoic and emotional. We have many "persons" within our heads while each is part of the whole.

Edward Stanford Martin captures the feeling of this inner multitude in his poem called "Mixed:"

> Within my earthly temple there's a crowd;
> There's one of us that's humble, one that's proud,
> There's one that's broken-hearted for his sins,
> And one that unrepentant sits and grins;
> There's one that loves his neighbors as himself,
> And one that cares for naught but fame and self,
> From much corroding care I should be free
> If I could once determine which is me![2]

The answer is simple. You have not one "me" to discover but a multitude to embrace. All the phases of your being are parts of you. Accept all of yourself—all the "me's"—and you shall be free of much of the inner turmoil. You see, a gentle embrace has a great quieting influence on your compounded consciousness.

You are a complex, compound expression of energies that often are at variance with one another. Stop worrying about it. That is the way you were intended. Stop denying parts of your being; instead, embrace your whole being. Realize more of your potential by affirming with Walt Whitman, "Do I contradict myself? Very well then, I contradict myself. (I am large. I contain multitudes.)"[3] Stop pushing yourself so hard. Stop berating yourself for inconsistencies. You contain multitudes.

However, let's get this in perspective. Your varied patterns of expression are not isolated—they are related. Each is a facet of the Cosmic expressing AS you and THROUGH you. You are first and foremost divine. Every person is. Divinity is the core of your plural selves. It is like sunlight, refracted through a prism which casts its rainbows in rich variety. Divinity not only differentiates between individuals, it differentiates widely through each individual. You contain "multitudes" because your divinity expresses that way.

You are the child of a King! Can you believe it? You are good and well-loved. Do you know it? You are an intricate mosaic of plural selves animated by Cosmic Power! Do you feel it? The psalmist sang that you are only a little lower than the angels. Jesus Christ said you are the salt of the earth. Yes, you are a god. You are so much more than what appears between your hat and your boots.

You have the power within you to transcend any limitation. A man by the name of Charles Fillmore said, "Man can never discern more than a segment of the circle in which he moves, although his powers and capacities are susceptible of infinite expansion . . . The farther he goes into mind the wider its horizon, until he is forced to acknowledge that he is not the personal, limited thing he appears, but the focus of an infinite idea."[4]

Now you have the authority to embrace yourself and surpass yourself. More correctly, I should say, you can embrace ALL yourselves (plural) and surpass ALL yourselves (plural). All the parts of you are expressions of the ONE-divinity. Look and see! You must be better than you have ever thought. Affirm all the varied selves of your interior household as legitimate expressions of God. It's all right to be you! As contradictory and complex as you often are, it's all right to be you.

Tolstoy captures this identity of oneness within the multitude of subpersonalities in this passage:

> One of the most widespread superstitions is that every man has his own special, definite qualities; that a man is kind, cruel, wise, stupid, energetic, apathetic, etc. Men are not like that . . . men are like rivers: the water is the same in each, and alike in all; but every river is narrow here, is more rapid there, here slower, there broader, now clear, now cold, now dull, now warm. It is the same with men. Every man carries in himself the germs of every human quality, and sometimes one manifests itself, sometimes another, and the man often becomes unlike himself, while still remaining the same man.[5]

The divine core of your being is always the same yet always varied in expression. This is the ground of your being. Thinking in this direction, you can accept a greater authority to direct your own life. Of your multiple selves, acknowledge the Cosmic Center. What's more, if you accept all the parts except the core, you are fragmented and confused. If you accept only the divine core and reject its varied expressions, you have denied important parts of your being. Seek to become grounded in your WHOLE BEING.

"Man must be arched and buttressed from within," wrote Marcus Aurelius, "else the temple wavers to the dust."[6] Life can be beautiful. You have the potential to make it anything you want. You have the inner authority to gather all the parts of yourself together. Between your hat and your boots is so very much! Begin to enjoy more of what's you.

Rollo May spoke once of the "courage of imperfection."[7] He was speaking of not being afraid to make mistakes. If a person is too careful, he will continually attempt to do only what he knows he can do well, which will limit him to doing tasks he has already tried. Hence, no reaching out and attempting something new and different will be possible. How wonderful to affirm a courage to do imperfectly, to dare to try something even if you may not do it very well.

However, there is another courage of imperfection. It takes courage to accept yourself as you are, with all the seeming faults and flaws. To courageously accept your own imperfectness creates the opposite experience from what you might expect. Rather than the apparent giving-in to mediocrity, you have opened the door for greatness. Only as you accept all the selves of you, as imperfect as many of them are, have you integrated your entire consciousness. So centered within all "yourselves," you can and will go forward.

Take comfort in this line from Emerson: "There is a crack in everything that God has made."[8] Nature is always in a state of becoming something-yet-more. You and I have flaws and "cracks"—we are ever in the process of becoming something-yet-more. How good it is to take a deep breath and decide it is good to be the imperfect expressions of God that we are. We are going forward from here. Yes, "There is a crack in everything that God has made."

A painter doing a portrait of famous Oliver Cromwell wanted to paint a perfect portrait. Cromwell said, "Paint me just as I am, warts and all."[9] That's it! Paint yourself just as you are. You are good! You are great! You are wonderful! Don't try to be more than what you are already; be more of what you are now. You will function better and accomplish more when you accept yourself as you are, "warts and all."

When you fight within yourself, your whole life seems to be in a turmoil. What a difference there is when you realize that your own definitions are all that can block you. You are putting yourself down when you could just as easily be putting yourself up. The start of putting yourself up is to be able to "put up" with yourself. Give yourself the love you need.

Carl Jung observed:

What I do unto the least of my brethren, that I do unto Christ. But what if I should discover that the least among them all, the poorest of all the beggars, the most impudent of all the offenders, the very enemy himself— that these are within me, and that I myself stand in need of the alms of my own kindness; that I myself am the enemy who must be loved—what then?[10]

Recognize that you are many subpersonalities, all in need of your own love. Start putting yourself up by putting up with yourself. Accept your "selves." Embrace yourself. Give yourself a kiss!

Dr. Irene Kassorla uses a simple exercise with many of her patients. She says to get quiet and close your eyes. Now kiss your finger tips and pat them against your cheeks. It's easy to do if you like yourself. And the more often you do it the more self-affirming it feels. Give yourself a kiss![11] You are a beggar, impudent, enemy, and you are funny, foolish, somewhat "cracked," with warts of one kind or another here and there. Yet, you are you and that is good. Give yourself a kiss!

Then give yourself a pat-on-the-back. Stretch your arm over your head as far as it will go and bring it down to your back. Give yourself a pat-on-the-back. By accepting yourself as you are, warts and all, you are embracing all the ways *God is living through you.* You are affirming your full divinity and with that you are well on the path to whatever you desire.

Here is another exercise you will enjoy. Roberto Assagiolo, M. D., created this activity he calls "The Dance of the Many Selves."[12] It works as a physical activity and is also valuable as an action only in your mind. In modified form, here it is:

(1) Stand in a place where you have room to move around. Breathe deeply and quietly relax. Now imagine that you are standing in the middle of a circle. All around the edge are your "subpersonalities" or the many different aspects of you. Explore each one in turn. You at the center are not critical, you are just experiencing consciously some of your many selves.

(2) Move into a subpersonality's place at the edge of the circle. Take on the body posture of that particular state of being. For example, if it was a frightened child, you might crouch down, hands over face; if it was a haughty queen or king, you might stand rigid and straight.

(3) Now exaggerate the posture and feel its quality and being in your body and feelings.

(4) Let a sound emerge that seems to go with this posture. The sound may be a word or only a sound.

(5) Make the sound several times, loudly. Feel that sound in your body.

(6) Now slowly leave the subpersonality and step back into the center. Become aware of your breathing again. Take on a posture of balance, calm, quiet. Then move into another subpersonality's place on the edge of the circle.

(7) Continue this exercise with as many parts of yourself as seem to present themselves. Now move, in your own time and rhythm, from the center into a subpersonality and back, creating a "dance" between the many selves and the center. Movements and sound will choreograph the dance into a powerful integrative experience. Then become quiet; return to the center.

Do the exercise right now. Work with it over a period of time until it becomes a delightful way of affirming your whole being. If you can't get into it, that's all right too. Go back and read these last two chapters again. Give yourself a kiss. Give yourself a pat-on-the-back. You are becoming grounded in your whole being. Embrace your whole self—from divinity through all the warts. The courage of imperfection is the path to becoming more of what you want to be. There's more to you than what's between your hat and your boots. Love it all. Give yourself a kiss.

CHAPTER SIX

Take Off Your Shoes

Get Comfortable Where You Are

When Moses saw the burning bush, he took off his shoes. That tradition continues today in several religions. If you have entered a mosque, you will recall that you were required to remove your shoes. In many cultures it is also a sign of respect when entering a private home to take off your shoes.

Historically, removing your shoes is an act of worship. It symbolizes removing your dusty or earthly thinking and becoming spiritually receptive. Besides, how much more comfortable you are! To take off your shoes is to open your mind to divinity. It is also an act of relaxing on the spot.

As we have seen earlier, you need to know where you are before you can get someplace else. Look at your thinking and feeling; then talk to yourself about what you see. Beyond your fears and doubts that need to be embraced before they can be healed, you have many selves or subpersonalities. You have embraced them too. The core of your being is the divine Presence. As you would get comfortable with all these rich dimensions of

49

yourself, get comfortable with your Real Self. Relax! You do not have to run anywhere. Take off your shoes!

You see, to be really grounded in yourself, you must be centered in all points of consciousness. If you affirm your divinity and deny the way divinity expresses through you, you are denying part of yourself. As you accept more of your whole self—even parts you have previously rejected and repressed, you are embracing more of the wholeness of Life As You. See yourself as integrated. Your core and your many selves are all connected to one another. Your previous grounding is a dimension of touching the Source. Now, *consciously* touch the Source. Open your mind to God; relax in Him.

The theologian Paul Tillich refers to God as "Ground of our very being." In *The Shaking of the Foundations* he writes: "The name of this infinite and inexhaustible depth and ground of being is God. That depth is what the word God means. And if that word has not much meaning to you, translate it, and speak of the depths of your life, of the source of your being, of your ultimate concern, of what you take seriously without reservation."[1]

That which is real and meaningful to you is the presence of God in your life. You are not alone. Your fears are ungrounded. Take off your shoes—let go of the limiting thoughts. God is the ground of your being. Get your head centered in this idea and you are strong, peaceful, confident and capable.

Take off your shoes! Get comfortable in the Presence of God that lives within you and all around you. Look and see that the place where you are now is good—is divine—is God. Elizabeth Browning voiced this truth with these famous lines:

Earth's crammed with heaven,
And every common bush afire with God;
But only he who sees takes off his shoes;
The rest sit round it and pluck blackberries.[2]

Too often we seek our God "somewhere else." We think our blessings lie ahead someplace. Right now is our good! Right here is our God! Every bush and every part of us is afire with God. Take off your shoes.

Look at it this way: The depths of your life—your ultimate concerns—are always with you. Within you are love, beauty, order, intelligence, care, faith, and joy. These enduring qualities you will always find when you look for them. You can see what you are prepared to see. If your thoughts have been blocking your vision of the Absolute, then get some new thoughts. God is there with you. Good is with you.

Certainly, everything that happens isn't good. There are obvious tragedies in the world. However, there is good within everything that happens. Often the good and the tragic are intertwined—we see the same situations differently, depending on which way our heads are going. We don't have to go so far as to try to find a "good reason" behind every happening. It is enough to find something of value even though the event is tragic.

Jacob decreed to the "angel" with whom he wrestled, "I will not let thee go except thou bless me." (Genesis 32:26) His challenge turned into a blessing. Sometimes the problems we complain about turn out to be "blessings in disguise" also. If we flee too quickly, we may miss the blessing. No matter how difficult a situation may be, we can look for some value, a blessing, any good. Those enduring values are always there.

Look for that "Ground of being" in every situation,

every event, every person. Emily Cady said, "The very circumstances of your life that seem heartbreaking evils will turn to joy before your very eyes if you will steadfastly refuse to see anything but God in them."[3] God is there if you will only look. Take off your blinders and see!

". . . They should seek the Lord, if haply they might feel after him, and find him, though he be not far from every one of us: For in him we live, and move, and have our being . . ." (Acts 17:27-28) As we take off the shoes of limited thinking, we see that Ground of being which is God. Then we do not feel alone or afraid. God is here; we live in Him. Every leaf is afire with God.

This concept is supported by modern science. The atomic theory explains each particle of the universe as a point of light surrounded by matter and held together by intelligence. Furthermore, matter and energy are interchangeable, governed by laws of intelligence. To describe the universe as intelligent energy is a good definition of God. He does not exist separate from His universe, but through it. We live, move, and have our being in the presence of the Absolute.

When I was a college student I discussed this idea with a professor of religion. He became upset with me and shouted, "Why, that's pantheism!" and would not talk to me further. I felt as though I had contracted measles. And I had to do some serious questioning and thinking about my beliefs, which is always good for any of us to do.

Christian theologians agree that God made the universe. This IS our Father's world, but traditional theology maintains that God made His world out of matter-separate-from-Himself and set it to working, and He frequently appears to have forgotten the whole thing. That line of logic also has a name; it is called teleology.

Now I believe with greater conviction than when I was in school that God is more than His universe, yet the same universe is God. You see, pantheism can mean a belief in many gods (which was perhaps what my friend the professor thought I meant) and it also describes a belief that God and the universe are one. Look at the universe around you. Every bush IS afire with God. There is no God AND the universe—there is only God AS the universe. We live in Him. We can see when we take off the shoes of limited beliefs.

Another limiting idea that needs to be removed from our understanding is the idea of opposites. We think in terms of polarity—good versus evil; health versus sickness; prosperity versus poverty; love versus hostility. No wonder we run with our fears. When we think this way, we also think we have to get someplace else—and quickly. On the other hand, when we see God in every situation, we can stand our ground. God is here now!

We live in God; every atom of the universe is God in expression. There can be no absence of the Absolute. Yet there are degrees of manifestation. The presence of God is constant even though we experience it in varying degrees. Sickness is not the opposite of health, it is a limited expression of omnipresent life. Poverty is a degree of manifest abundance. Depression is a degree of expressed joy. There are no opposites. There is only God.

We can feel cold and we can see that the night sky is dark. That is certainly the appearance. However, these appearances are relative expressions of the Absolute. From the standpoint of engineering, there is no "cold." There is only heat expressed to some degree. Refrigeration does not make anything cold—it is a process of removing heat. In the same way, there is no darkness—only some degree of light. A light meter measures the amount of light present. There can always be a greater or lesser degree. There is always light.

Hate and love are not opposites—they are in fact similar and often confused within an individual. Each is a degree of concern about something or someone. Apathy is a limited degree of concern. Love and hate are increased levels of the same concern. There are no opposites. Look at every common bush and see! God is with you; you can stand your ground!

From this perspective, there are no negatives in the universe except unfulfilled positives. What appears as an absence is a limited manifestation of abundance. Every problem is but the unripened state of good. Negation is nothing more than arrested development. It is difficult only if you stop there. Don't stop! Fulfill your state of health named "sickness" into greater life. Expand your poverty into greater abundance. Ripen the negative into its intended positive. This you can do from the perspective of your Ground of being. Even as you have embraced all the facets of your own expression, embrace the fullness of God. Before you seek to solve by prayer and action, get centered in God. *Stop-Think!* Stop and think into the place where you now stand. Get comfortable in God where you are now.

We can talk about knowing the whole world, but we can only know that part of the world which we personally experience. How can we comprehend the entire ocean? We can't—it is too large to grasp. Yet we can go swimming at one beach and experience that part of the ocean.

In the same way, the Absolute is much too extensive for us to understand. But we know God in our own experience. Only here, where we now stand, can we feel the Ground of being.

Take the shoes off your feet—literally and figuratively. Run barefoot through God's world; wiggle your toes in His sand. As you look at yourself and that part of the world in which you stand, see with a new vision that God is with you. Experience that vision more fully. It is imperative, because to know the presence of God is basic to your personal success.

Success is being comfortable in your environment. That's where success starts. You can never swim while you are still fighting the water. Relax! You are in your element. Take the shoe-like limits off your head and see that God (Good) is in you and you are in God (Good).

Such a perspective has ecological benefits too. As we see the world as an expression of the same divinity as ourselves we care for it, respect our milieu, protect and preserve our environment. Everything becomes more sacred as we see God in it.

Those personal fears that plague us begin to dissolve when we feel surrounded in God. There is no need to run—there is no better place to run. No longer seeing opposites, we settle into the ground of our being with a quiet peace. Whatever we want more of, we shall have—not something "other" than where we are right now, but as an extension of the good we now have. Right here is a good place.

Now you have looked at negatives and invited them into a dance. You know that God was there all the time. You stopped and looked and talked to yourself about what was happening in your consciousness. Then you inserted that wedge of silence and watched it widen and fill your being with peace. You have even given yourself a kiss and danced with the many subpersonalities of your being. In all these ways you have been grounding yourself—centering your energies to form an integrity from which you can be and do what you choose.

These same exercises can be applied to the very Ground of being—the God-core of yourself. You were celebrating God (Good) at every turn. Stop! Look! Talk! Quiet! Here are four steps with which to center yourself. *Stop:* relax and be still. Be comfortable and quiet. Actually take off your shoes and let go. *Look:* to the center of your being and of every particle of the world around you. God is there. See that every common bush is afire with Divinity. *Talk:* to yourself about this Omnipresence. Say out loud, "Wherever I am, God is." Say it now. Add, "In God I live, move, and have my being. I am never alone for God is with me. Every bush is alive with Him. I have nothing to fear for God is with me." *Quiet:* relax and trust the place in God where you are now. In four simple steps, you are grounded in your many selves and, most importantly, grounded in your God-self.

Additionally, a daily practice of seeing your immediate world with new vision helps you to experience your Ground of being. As you would actually run barefoot through life and feel the different textures of God's earth, taste and see that God is everywhere around you. Look for God (Good) in every situation.

Take off your shoes! Relax right where you are, for "here" is good. See that every place is a God-place of holy ground. Remove the old concepts that would make you fear or run. Don't rush anywhere; be still. Wiggle your toes in the sands of God that are now under your feet. You are grounded in your own being and now grounded in the very Ground of your being. Earth's crammed with heaven, and now you know it. *Stop-Think-Start!* Your grounding builds a center from which to achieve. Now your prayers, affirmations, and meditations will work as never before.

PART THREE

Stop—Think—Start!
The Law of Substitution

CHAPTER SEVEN

Displace; Replace; Substitute!

Your Head Goes One Way at a Time

The most important thing we can learn is to control our thoughts. The purpose of all educational purposes is the development of the ability to think. Thinking is our most important asset. Man's ability to think is the greatest feature that evolution has bestowed. As we continue to evolve, we will do so through thought control. Charles Darwin, famous scientist, wrote, "The highest possible stage in moral culture is when we recognize that we ought to control our thoughts."[1]

Thoughts can be controlled! If you would like to think differently from the way you now think, you can do it. Displace; replace; substitute! Displace the hold that fear and worry have on you by replacing any unwanted thought with a desired one. It's the practical law of substitution.

The lyrics of an old song say, "You gotta accentuate the positive, eliminate the negative."[2] It's a simple way of stating this law. Your mind can entertain only one thought at a time. You can't have two thoughts simultaneously. Thoughts can change so quickly that you may

61

not have realized it, but, whether you like it or not, you have a one-track mind. So does everyone else.

Think about something—anything. During that thought you cannot think of anything else. Thoughts occupy your head, one at a time. If you are entertaining something positive, you can't be thinking something negative. If you fink yourself thinking something that upsets you, decide to think about something else. The negative thought can't get through. As with the telephone, if you keep the telephone-line of your mind busy with positive, creative thoughts, then fears and worries will always get a busy signal. They might, in fact, eventually forget your number. By accentuating the positive, you do eliminate the negative.

Life is that experience of thought forever flowing through your head. Stop; refuse to think on that which makes you unhappy. Start thinking what you want to think. Then you are using the law of substitution—you are replacing something you don't want with something you do want. It's simply a matter of what you accentuate. There are bound to be both negative and positive things in your world. You can see them all, but you do not have to accentuate and emphasize that which is negative in your life.

This law of substitution works on many levels. This chapter applies the law on a primary mental level. It is imperative to grasp this application before going on. The rest of this section amplifies the principle to affirmative prayer, creative disciplines, and physical activities which promote success. The entirety of this text expands the law of substitution through imaginative faith and deeper experiences in prayer. The law works!

However, if it doesn't seem to be working for you at any point, stop and get centered. You may be moving ahead too fast. Substitution does not work well as an avoidance game. Whenever your head is not going the way you would like for it to go, alternate your substitutions with intermittent centering on where you are. You must be centered in the current working of your consciousness before your forward strides will be effective. Back up in your mind and get grounded in yourself. Look, listen, and talk to yourself more closely. As you know where you are, your substitutions will work to move you forward.

The law of substitution is the way you control your thoughts. You need this control because everything in your life depends on the thoughts you think. Think what you want to think; eliminate the negative. Get rid of what you don't want. Emmet Fox said, "Negative thoughts and feelings are like a spark that falls on your coat sleeve. Brush it off and it will do no damage. Let it linger and it will burn a hole."[3]

As you dwell on what you don't want, that is what you are accentuating. That becomes your attitude, which is fully 90 percent of your experience! An old Chinese proverb says, "You cannot prevent the birds of sadness from flying over your head, but you can prevent them from nesting in your hair." It's up to you to brush off that spark, to select your own thoughts. There are all kinds of conditions in the world, but you decide what you nurture, what you emphasize, what you think about the majority of the time. You decide what "builds its nest in you." Your mind can go only one way at a time. You decide what it will be!

We all have had days when some unwanted incident occurred and we ignorantly allowed it to turn our day into a shambles. Just when you were ready to leave, the car would not start. Your best friend did something that seems terribly unkind. In the middle of your favorite program, the television station went off the air. A competitive company has just succeeded in taking over one of your major accounts. You bought a new coat; when you got it home you found a tear in the lining. None of these misfortunes is necessarily a catastrophe, but if you let your mind go undisciplined, you can turn it into one. You can think yourself from a minor frustration through a gamut of emotions that concludes in anger or depression.

I remember reading a story years ago called, "Wanna Borrow a Jack?" A man was driving in the country late at night when one of the tires on his car went flat. He had a spare tire but no jack. It seemed the only thing to do was to walk back to the nearest farmhouse and borrow a jack. On the walk he talked to himself: "It's so late they will be asleep. They won't like a stranger who awakens them. Since they don't know me, why would they trust me with their jack? Maybe they don't even have one. Out of meanness, they might refuse."

He rang the bell, and had worked himself into such a state that when the door was answered he shouted, "I don't want your silly jack anyway!"

The best way to prevent such self-caused miseries is to stop them before they get started. To "nip it in the bud" is easier than working yourself out of a self-imposed fit. The sooner the negative course of thought is stopped the better it is for you.

There is always a point within the inner dialogue that

is like a fork in the road. Your thoughts can lead either way. What usually happens is you don't recognize what is happening until you are already angry or depressed. The secret is to watch your thoughts more closely to recognize the pivotal point. The miseries that start in your own head are best solved when caught before or as they start. To do this, learn to interrupt your mind.

When you want to replace one kind of thought with another, it is necessary to displace the authority of the current thought. Your *Start-Think!* requires a strong stop! A firm "No" can do the trick. Tell yourself, "No! No, I will not think that way!" Think—Stop! and really STOP!

Judge Thomas Troward, a great teacher of metaphysics, instructed his students how to effect such a stop in an enjoyable way. He said to say silently, "Cock-a-doodle-do" to any unwanted state of mind. I think it helps to say it out loud too. Thinking or saying it is so ridiculous that you will often laugh, which helps you all the more to really STOP. Troward wrote, "To 'Cock-a-doodle-do' at any suggestion is to treat it with scorn and derision, and to assume the very opposite of that receptive attitude which enables a suggestion to affect us."[4] A firm "no" is a positive help in shifting gears.

Dr. Wallace Wilkins,[5] a psychologist, is nationally known for his success with desensitization and therapy to conquer phobias. He says, "It is impossible to be relaxed and anxious at the same time." Again, the mind can entertain only one direction at a time. He teaches that one technique in overcoming fear is to make the mind change signals. For example, a loud noise will shift attention away from the fear to the noise. Essentially, you tend to forget about what you were thinking. Some of his patients have learned to clap their hands loudly or snap their fingers when they detect the start of fear. One woman wore a rubber-band on her wrist. When she felt panic coming on, she would snap it. It must have hurt her, but it kept her attention away from her fear.

Obviously, there are times and places where a loud clap of your hands or a vocal "Cock-a-doodle-do" would not be appropriate. "But," says Dr. Wilkins, "anyone can shout inside his own head, 'Stop!' It works quite well." Sound familiar? The secret of mind control is to be able to interrupt any mental signal at will. Clap your hands, shout out loud, say "Stop!" Once you realize you are off the track you can interrupt that direction of thought. Stop your current "think" and think-STOP!

My friend Eric Butterworth tells about a little girl who had just hurt her knee and yet was enduring pain without crying. Her mother asked her how she could be so brave. She replied, "I just say to myself, 'Stop that!' and make myself mind me."[6] Whatever you need to stop thinking, you can. Tell yourself, "Stop that!" and make yourself mind you.

Another way to interrupt negative ruminations in your head is to ask yourself these three specific questions: (1) Whose problem is this? (2) What can I do about it now? (3) If I can't do anything else, how can I distract myself? A question is a new challenge. It is a good way to *Stop-Think!* so as to really *Start-Think!* Let's look at these three more closely.

(1) "Whose problem is this?" Many of your concerns are not your own. You may be fretting over what someone else has to decide. You make your life a muddle

when you try to solve other people's problems in addition to your own. Sometimes, you are still "parenting" your children when they are old enough to think for themselves. It just isn't your business any more.

(2) "What can I do about it now?" Anxieties are related to inactivity. You might be upset because you should be doing something. The longer you delay, the more you procrastinate, the more tense you become. Patience is a virtue, but not when you should be busy. I recently found this advice on the tag to my tea bag, "Patience is not always a virtue—certainly not when you are in quicksand." What can you do about what is bothering you?

If your health is a concern, go to the doctor and find out what should be done. If you're worried about your job, try doing it better, set about learning the additional skills you obviously need, or start looking for new employment. If you are lonely, go out and meet somebody. If you don't know what you can do, seek someone who can give you good advice. (Of course, in all of these areas, you can turn within to that presence of God; we'll talk more about that later.) Better than worrying about your investments is to talk to your lawyer, trust officer, tax expert, stock broker, or insurance agent. There are usually so many things you can do right away and often there are experts you can turn to for advice.

(3) "How can I distract myself?" There are circumstances when you know that the problem is your own and you have done everything you can for the moment. If you can't do anything constructive about the problem, be sure you are not making it worse. At least get into

neutral. Clap your hands, give forth with numerous "Cock-a-doodle-do's" to create a diversion. Go for a walk. Watch television or go to a movie. Pick up your knitting or go fix that leaking faucet. Have an absorbing novel handy and get lost in it. Write your mother-in-law a letter—she will be delighted. Whatever you do, make sure the old worry has come to a screeching halt. *Stop-Think!*

In a book on psychological techniques by David Knox is explained a technique of thought control called "Stop-think:"

> This procedure involves the client interrupting his negative thoughts and substituting a more positive set of ideas. A female client recently noted that she felt extremely fearful of being home alone at night when her husband was out of town. The stop-think technique was used in that she was instructed to say to herself, "Stop," when she became aware of various ruminations concerning the possibility of someone breaking in . . . When she said, "Stop," she was to get an index card out of her purse or drawer on which was written a number of pleasurable statements, i.e., she and her husband are very pleased with the recent grandchild, she and her husband will go to Miami for a vacation in the spring, their son is healthy and happy and has recently graduated with honors in a most promising field.
>
> In effect, the negative pattern is being interrupted and substituted by thoughts incompatible with anxiety or unhappiness. This particular technique works well with most any type of mental compulsion in which the individual continues to ruminate about negative happenings. In effect, the cycle of these ruminations is broken.[7]

Only one thought can occupy your mind at a time. If that thought which is occupying your mind is not producing the kind of attitudes and results that you want, then you can easily substitute it. Say to yourself, "Stop" when you become aware of negative "ruminations." Then think about something that is pleasurable and meaningful in your life.

Here's how it works. First of all, make a list of enjoyable thoughts. Put them on index cards to fit your purse or billfold. When you are aware of a negative rumination starting (or if you've been slow and recognize it is already in full-swing) apply the law of substitution. Say to yourself, "Stop!" Then get out your list of creative ideas. You might have written about your new baby, your next vacation, the possible raise in salary, past accomplishments, personal successes. Then you displace the hold your fear has over you; replace it with thoughts of a rewarding nature, and literally eliminate the negative by substituting the positive.

It works! It works best when you start it close to the pivotal point in mind where you go off the track. If you go way out on that negative path and get into a fit of anger or depression it is more difficult to start substituting thoughts. But it will still work. Have your list of positive ideas handy. Get that list out and literally force yourself, if necessary, to think in the way that you want to think. Turn around and go the other way. Think in a new direction.

This is what Jesus was saying when we read in Luke, "I tell you but except ye repent ye shall perish." (Luke 13:3) When we hear the word "repent" we often think of an oldfashioned kind of religion of damnation and hell-fire. Actually the word means in its original Greek "change your thought." That means, turn around and go the other way. Think in a new direction. Except you change your mind you shall perish—you shall have misfortunes and unhappiness. Think a new thought and you will think in a new direction. Until you think differently, you're going to stay in the same unpleasant condition.

The only thing you ever need to change is yourself. You can control your thinking; that's the way you change yourself! Repent; turn around and go the other way. Think into something that is more creative and more worthwhile. Use the law of substitution. Displace; replace; substitute!

When you are sick or unhappy, you still choose your thoughts. When problems are piled high, you only compound them when you think about nothing else. Your choice is to repent or perish. Think a new thought about yourself. Think a new thought about your life. Change the direction of your thinking and you will change your experience.

Emily Cady says in *Lessons in Truth,* "If you turn your thoughts away from the external toward the spiritual, and let them dwell on the good in yourself and others, (substitution) all the apparent evil will first drop out of your thoughts and then out of your life."[8] You can, by practice, learn to make your mind be still. Let the mind that is God's think in and through you. You can control your thoughts and thereby control your attitude and your life.

Another way of expressing the principle is to "ignore

the inconsequential!'' It sounds good, but it's impossible to do. Try it. Ignore the inconsequential! What's happening? The more you think about the inconsequential that you're going to ignore, you're not ignoring it, you're giving it more attention. The only way you can ignore the inconsequential is to think about the consequential. Get your mind on the substitute—that which you want to think about. Spiritual concepts such as Bible passages, yoga, or mantras, are important substitutions. We'll consider the importance of spiritual thinking later. Right now, apply the law of substitution to equal alternatives. If one thought makes you unhappy and another thought lifts you up, choose the better of the two. Even if it only makes you feel better, that is a good reason. This is a level of application that can be a transition to prayer or an end in itself. Consider it first as an end result. It's a matter of repenting—of getting a new thought about yourself, about life or about anything else.

The birds of unhappiness fly over us all; you don't have to allow them to nest in your hair. Life is what you make it, and you make it what it is by the choice of your own thoughts. *Stop-Think!* It's all in your head. Use the law of substitution: displace; replace; substitute! Brush off the spark before it does any damage. Then *Start-Think!*

When the negative ruminations start within you, interrupt them. The closer to their starting point you call out your "Stop," the easier it will be. Nip fear in the bud. Clap your hands. Snap a rubber-band on your wrist. Tell yourself quietly or aloud, "Stop!" Affirm numerous "Cock-a-doodle-do's." Ask yourself some confrontative questions: Whose problem is this? What can I do about it now? How can I distract myself? Is your *Stop-Think!* list ready for use, put on an index card? Displace the hold any fear has on you by replacing unwanted thoughts with desired ones. *Stop-Think!* Stop thinking what you don't want to think. *Start-Think!* Think what you choose to think. It's the law of substitution, and it works! *Displace; Replace; Substitute!*

CHAPTER EIGHT

Talk Up to Yourself

Convince Yourself; Encourage Yourself!

Some years ago, a young man was talking to himself in the desert. "My book is going to be a success," he said. "It will be bought by the Book-of-the-Month Club. A prominent movie studio will buy the movie rights. I'll make so much money from this book that I'll be able to buy a brand-new Chrysler . . ."[1] The desert plants within hearing apparently made little response, but he responded to himself. His pep-talk came true!

The man was Thomas Duncan, author of *Gus the Great*, *Big River*, and *Virgo Descending*. All of these novels have been successful. Most successful was *Gus the Great,* which he was writing at the time of his speech to himself in the desert. He said in an interview, "Each morning I used to go out and give my little speech to the seemingly empty air of the desert. And each day I used to write down the things I wanted . . ." Every one of his predictions came true. The movie rights were leased to Universal-International for $167,500. He says, "You have to sell yourself the idea that something is within your reach. Then you can achieve it."

73

The French sage Pascal advises, "Man holds an inward dialogue with himself that it behooves him to regulate very well."[2] You can monitor and control the inner dialogue instead of letting it meander aimlessly. When your mind is talking nonsense, you can say, "Stop!" You, and only you can change the direction. Think in a new direction! Speak to yourself in a way that lifts you up.

In one of Lewis Carroll's books, the White Queen taught Alice this same truth:

> "Oh, don't go on like that!" cried the poor Queen, wringing her hands in despair. "Consider what a great girl you are. Consider what a long way you've come today. Consider what o'clock it is. Consider anything, but don't cry!"
>
> Alice could not help laughing at this, even in the midst of her tears. "Can you keep from crying by considering things?" she asked.
>
> "That's the way it's done," the Queen said with great decision: "nobody can do two things at once, you know."[3]

Such considering of things is a good way to keep your thoughts going the way you want them to go. Talk to yourself in a way that gets your life going forward.

Now, talking to yourself is sometimes suspect. We hear that it's all right, as long as you don't answer yourself. We tease one another that the "men in the white coats" will be coming for you. It can be embarassing when someone overhears you in a verbal exchange with yourself. Years ago I solved that situation. Whenever I'm caught talking to and with myself I reply, "That's all right. This way I know I have an intelligent listener!"

It breaks the possible tension and gives me a pat on the back. Do the same thing!

It is a fact that we talk to ourselves all of the time. The inward dialogue goes on constantly, even if we ourselves are unaware of it. Because life is all in our heads, we are eternally "considering" things. Some people talk to themselves "positively awful." Others talk to themselves "awfully positive." What will it be for you? Talk up to yourself and that's the way your life will go. What you speak about, you think about. What you think about, you bring about.[4]

As Emerson said more than one hundred years ago, "Every thing the individual sees without him corresponds to his states of mind."[5] Your thoughts produce you, and you produce your thoughts. Since the dialogue is going on all of the time, why not talk up to yourself?

You can interrupt any pattern of inner conversation; you can also start any new dialogue you choose. However, be sure you are moving in the right direction. One man went to his minister for help. He had many health problems and in a short while it was evident to the minister that this man was excessively negative. The minister invited the man to affirm twenty times a day, "Each day I am healthier and healthier."

The man returned in a week looking and feeling worse. His complaint this time was that he couldn't use the affirmation very well because he kept losing count. The minister said, "Take a string and tie twenty knots in it. Every time you say the statement move your fingers to another knot and you won't have to count." The man was pleased and left. When he came back the third time he was worse than ever.

"What are you doing?" asked the minister.

"Just what you told me," said the man. "I say twenty times a day, 'Each day I am healthier and healthier, knot. Each day I am healthier and healthier, knot. Each day . . .' "

He was negating every positive statement he made. Obviously, the unconscious mind is not concerned with spelling. If you say, "I am healthy, not" you will not be talking up to yourself. The kind of application you want is one that will encourage and uplift.

Dr. Bernard Berkowitz and Dr. Mildred Newman created a best-seller, *How To Be Your Own Best Friend*. They say, "It's important to learn to listen to ourselves . . . If we learn how to listen, we will find out a lot and we will hear some wonderful things."[6] We may hear some wonderful things and we may hear some frightening things. All control depends on our monitoring ability to first listen to ourselves. When we hear what we don't want to hear, we can change it.

These authors continue, "You must also learn to talk to yourself. That's very important. You need to explain things, to reassure yourself. You need to establish an on-going dialogue. It can help you through all kinds of tough situations . . . there is usually a moment when it could go either way. If you pay attention, you can take that moment and consider what you really want to do. You have the power to stop yourself; this is a good thing to know. At first it's hard, but it gets easier."[7]

There is that pivotal place where the inner dialogue can go either way. The more you are in touch with yourself, the sooner you will recognize that place. Then it is easier to substitute what you want to think. Did you catch the phrase, "You must also learn to talk to yourself?" We talk all of the time—sometimes with inhibition, and often with lots of fear and negation. As we learn to talk to ourselves, we catch ourselves thinking in unwanted directions and change the inner dialogue to "consider" something desired.

Every thought you entertain becomes one of the events of your life. When you change one thought, it doesn't seem to make too much difference. What you're seeking to do is change the average standard of your thoughts. If you have a tub of water at 70° and you add one glass of 90° water, you won't change the tub temperature very much. But the more 90° water you add, the more you will raise the temperature. So it is with the mind. The more you substitute the thoughts you want by telling yourself encouraging, healing words, the more your mental temperature changes. In other words, regular pep-talks are necessary to keep your consciousness where you want it.

A successful salesman told me that all high-level salesmen talk to themselves all day long. A salesman answers the objections he might hear. He reminds himself that many of his best sales started with a "No" from the customer. He keeps telling himself what he needs to hear for two reasons: First, he drowns out the unwanted voices, and second, he builds his case to succeed.

Keep talking to yourself all day long. Talk yourself up to yourself. Build yourself up; encourage yourself. What you speak about, you think about. What you think about, you bring about.

Think and talk to yourself about your dreams, your plans, your goals. Tell yourself the tenets of faith that inspire and lift you. Remind yourself that you are a child of God and can do whatever you need to do. You can do anything you believe in. Believe in yourself. By talking to yourself in this way, you are preparing for your success. In the words of Emerson, "To think is to act."[8] Your thoughts are actions that lead to your success.

In Matthew, Mark, and Luke there is the account of the woman who had been hemorrhaging for many years. In Matthew we read this version, "And, behold, a woman, which was diseased with an issue of blood twelve years, came behind him, and touched the hem of his garment: For she said within herself, If I may but touch his garment, I shall be whole." (Matthew 9:20–21) The healing took place after she said to herself it was possible. That's the way it always works. What we say to ourselves is what happens!

Jesus reinforced this interpretation by telling the woman that she was healed by her own faith. Because she believed in healing, it happened. Faith is generated by the inner dialogue. What we mentally rehearse is the substance of faith. Learn to talk to yourself with faith, encouragement, health, and success.

An article about Jerry LeVias of the Houston Oilers says he talked himself into successful football. At five-foot nine and one-hundred and seventy pounds, he is smaller than most men in his sport. He also had had polio. His family tried to talk him out of such a rough sport. However, "Jerry LeVias talks to himself, and he talks big."

LeVias told himself, "The way to avoid being crushed is to be always in motion. Never take two steps in the same direction." He repeatedly described to himself a situation where he could jump for a long, game-winning pass in the final seconds of the game. Eight times in college football he pulled it off, just like his inner rehearsal, and went on to professional football. A small man had talked himself into being a star in a big man's game.[9]

One spring in Tampa, Florida, a teen-aged youth jacked up his automobile and crawled beneath it to work on the car. Suddenly, the jack slipped and the car fell on him. He yelled for help and his parents came running. The father reasoned that no human being could cope with a 3,500-pound car, so he reached for the jack. The mother, who had been ill and weighed only 123 pounds, reached for the rear bumper and lifted the car straight into the air. Later she said, "I only knew that I had to save my boy."[10] She talked to herself. She told herself what to do and she did it.

Talk to yourself like that. So fill yourself with the greater, there is no room for the lesser. Tell yourself you can help. You can be healed. You can succeed. When you hear yourself putting yourself down, *Stop-Think!* Then *Start-Think!* Push yourself up! Say things like this: "Each day I am healthier and healthier. Every day in every way I am better and better. I have a healthy body and it is going to stay that way. The mark of success is upon me. I can do what I must do. I am always successful in everything I do. My disposition comes from God and is joyous! I feel wonderful and I share my joy with the world around me." Begin each day by saying, "I can! I can! I can! I believe! I believe! I believe! I will! I will! I will!"

Any thought that pushes you up is using the law of

substitution to go forward. You can expand yourself to be more and to have more. Judge Troward said, "It is a mathematical truism that you cannot contract the infinite, and that you can expand the individual . . ."[11] Every word that lifts you up expands you into more of the infinite. The more you make yourself aware of the possibility of an idea, the more likely that idea will assert itself.

Talk to the desert. Talk to the walls. Talk to yourself. Learn to listen to yourself and to talk to yourself. Don't worry about what other people will say. When they see the growth in you they will start doing the same thing. What you speak about, you think about. What you think about, you bring about. For at least one month, set a daily time to give yourself regular pep-talks.

Others have talked themselves into better lives and so can you. Convince yourself; encourage yourself. "You can! You believe! You will!" Think on these things and they will result in your life. *Stop-think* to *Start-Think!* Use the law of substitution, and talk up to yourself.

CHAPTER NINE

Act in Cold Blood

Doing Generates Power

Start-Think! is for your body as well as your mind. Even when you have decided to substitute pleasant thoughts for negative ones, gone further to speak affirmations to expand yourself into more of God, and committed yourself to the disciplines necessary to attain your good, you still have to put yourself into gear. Someone quipped that today "it is easier to organize a conference on the quality of the environment than to stoop over and pick up a gum wrapper."[1] At some point you have to want a new way of life enough to do something about it. Go after it!

We all get "cerebral." We have something we want to do but we bog down in the head. It isn't the work itself that overwhelms us, it's thinking about it. The project seems more difficult the longer we look at it. We sometimes talk ourselves out of what we seek. There are many excuses for inaction, and they all leave us right where we started or worse. We must get "out of our heads" and into our living.

The German poet-philosopher Goethe wrote years ago:

81

> Lose this day loitering, it will be the same story
> Tomorrow, and the rest more dilatory;
> Thus indecision brings its own delays
> And days are lost tormenting over other days.[2]

This can all be changed. Get started. Don't think about it so much and start moving! Don't try to figure out all the angles, move your feet. Don't try so hard to have both security and success at the same time, decide to get going. It's all in your head, to be sure, and don't let it stay there. Move your body and you change your head.

Carlyle wrote, ". . . lay this other precept well to heart, which to me was of invaluable service: *'Do the Duty which lies nearest thee,'* which thou knowest to be a Duty! Thy second Duty will already have become clearer."[3] That is to say, *doing generates power.* When you start something, you set into motion the power to complete it. Emerson said it this way, "Do the thing and you shall have the power."[4] Don't wait any longer. *Start-Think!* and act in cold blood!

The natural law of inertia states that (1) objects at rest tend to remain at rest, and (2) objects in motion tend to remain in motion. Applying this law to yourself, if you are sitting still, you will tend to continue doing nothing. Conversely, once you begin, you have the potential of success on your side. Doing generates power.

Henry David Thoreau said so wonderfully, "If one advances confidently in the direction of his dreams, and endeavors to live the life which he has imagined, he will meet with success unexpected in common hours."[5] Get started. Get the law of inertia going for you and you can reach whatever goal you have set. Substitute action for inaction and you are over half-way home.

What do you want most today? Start the wheels rolling right now. Put your book down and do something. Now! Telephone a specialist. Write that letter for information. Go to the library. Put your house up for sale. Go to the nearest university and find out about day and night courses. Move! Begin! Act! Start! Get going!

Have you done something? You have set causes moving that generate results. You have done the thing and you have the power. No longer are you only "cerebral"— wishing and thinking. You have taken action. This advertisement appeared recently for the United States Navy, "Life is too short to waste time wishing you were somewhere else. Get moving."[6] Whether you're joining the armed services or joining the stream of life, get moving and keep moving. Action, substituted for inaction, leads to answers.

I love this line from Nietzsche, "We think with our bodies. All truths are bloody truths to me. No truth is true but that it is thought in the open air."[7] In the game of life it is always your move. So, get started. Put into practice what you have learned and what you believe. Your philosophies will live and breathe as you do. Think with your whole body and get going.

Whenever you are saturated in unwanted emotions, action of some kind provides a physical substitution that will clear your head. Go take a walk. Someone said that there is no fear in the world that can survive a walk around the block. Just such a simple action as walking is a mighty one to move you where you want to go.

When Robert Frost, our great American poet, was a college freshman, his fraternity brothers worried about his long walks in the woods. A delegation of seniors confronted him and asked him what he did walking by himself in the woods. Frost looked at them and replied, "Gnaw bark." Thereafter, they left him alone.[8]

Actually, when Robert Frost took his walks, he was thinking and meditating. He continued that practice throughout his life. Just the action of taking a walk can neutralize almost any undesirable emotion. Start moving toward your goal; at least take a walk to clear your consciousness. Taking a walk can be a simple substitution of action that will lead to your success.

You see, doing something physical provides you with power to continue going forward, and it also gives you further direction. When you act, you change your perspective. Progress provides alternatives that couldn't be seen from the sidelines. You refine your objectives by starting out in some direction. By moving from point "A" to point "B" you have a new horizon. You can now see new alternatives. You may go on to "C" or "pass Go and collect $200.00.'"[9] As you go, you can see more ways to go. It's simple!

Jesus referred to the kingdom of heaven as a net " . . . that was cast into the sea, and gathered of every kind: Which, when it was full, they drew to shore, and sat down, and gathered the good into vessels, but cast the bad away." (Matthew 13:47–48) Heaven is an expanding consciousness of good. You are in heaven as your mind is opening up to more alternatives. Yet, that expanding mind is not only receptive, it is also selective. The more you do, the more you will see to do. After you start an action you will refine it, and cast away that which doesn't serve you. Progress provides alternatives. The more you move, the more you will see; the more you see, the more you can choose.

Purportedly, Xenophanes, the Greek soldier and writer, wrote, "The gods do not reveal everything to a man from the beginning, but by searching men find out in time what is best." Ask, seek, knock! Action gives power; action gives direction! The thing to do is set up goals, no matter how impossible they may seem, and start moving toward them. Act in cold blood!

Bob McCallister is a professional world-changer. He's a salesman's salesman, creating amazing success and teaching others to do the same. He says, "Every successful salesman changes the business climate around him every day of his life."[10]

Picture the situation according to McCallister. The successful salesman is responsible for one-half million dollars of sales each year. Yet, his customers are always in the midst of a cost-control program. The *Wall Street Journal* is full of gloomy news, and the buyer's desk has a fresh memo reminding him to hold down all purchases. Into this gloom walks the good salesman. A good order may have eluded him for a week, yet he exudes an aura of success. His whole manner suggests he's fresh from companies on the way up. He radiates the news that things are going well with him and you'd better get on board.

He might do this ten or twelve times a day. At the end of the day he has left a trail of optimism in his wake that wasn't there before. Five days a week he does this, literally changing the economic climate in his part of the world. This is the life of Bob McCallister and it can be yours. Act in cold blood!

That's what William James says: "We need only in cold blood to act as if the thing in question were real and it will infallibly end by growing into such a connection with our life that it will become real."[11] You pray with your whole being when you get your truths out in the open air. All truths are "bloody truths" and when you act on them in cold blood you accomplish your intentions. *Start-Think!* Substitute ACTION for inaction.

The way you act, the momentum you create, the causes you set into motion, all bring you certain feelings. Your thinking makes you depressed. Then your depression makes you think more of the same. Your body and mind keep "talking" back and forth to each other and the vicious cycle is on. But there is a way out. You think you tremble because you are afraid, but by trembling you make yourself afraid.[12] Your actions speak to your head. What you say with your body will speak loudly to your head. Stop trembling, and your head won't be afraid. Stand tall, and you speak to yourself of confidence. Sit in a relaxed position, and you tell your mind that you are peaceful. What is more, you will not only be telling yourself something important, you will be influencing everyone around you!

You can walk into the office and change the economics. The way you walk, the way you smile, the way you talk, the way you handle your money will change the situation. You can enter your own front door and change the situation of love right there. Your interest, your joy, and your friendship will be infectious. Act in cold blood with your bloody truths.

The thing to do is set up your goals and start moving toward them. Even if you're only going through the motions—faking it—to get the momentum started. Again, favorite words from Goethe, "I find the great thing in this world, is not so much where we stand, as in what direction we are moving." He continues with words you could put on a card and look at every day: "Are you in earnest? Seize this very minute! Whatever you can do or dream you can begin it! Boldness has genius, power and magic in it!"

If you would have more faith, step out; walk with confidence. If you would have more health, act healthy. Pray with your whole body and substitute healthy behavior. If you would be prosperous, act as if you had money. Dress up and look like a million! Create your own climate of whatever you seek. The law of inertia always acts for you. Life goes the way you are going. When you begin, you will receive the power to finish. Doing generates power.

Your head can go only one way at a time. Displace; replace; substitute! Interrupt the negative ruminations as soon as possible, and start talking up to yourself. Use the law of substitution to get your whole body in motion. Doing generates power. Move! Begin! Act! Start! Get going! *Start-Think!* Act in cold blood, now!

PART FOUR

Stop—Think—Start!
The Lure of Empty Categories

CHAPTER TEN

The Open Invitation

Reality Is Organic

Lao-Tzu, the Chinese philosopher, probably lived in the sixth century B. C. He is credited with writing the religious classic, the *Tao Te Ching,* although modern authorities believe the book was written several hundred years later. One of the concepts contained in that book is the importance of spaces. "The Tao is an empty vessel; it is used, but never filled. Oh, unfathomable source of ten thousand things."[1]

At first it is a strange idea to our western minds. We see a vase or a house as "a thing" for use. Yet the use of each is dependent on emptiness. The vase can be filled because it is open. The sides, which we see, create the space which we cannot see. This space is a capacity to be filled. The house has form, but it is within the space it creates that we find shelter. The openings to the house are empty yet they provide access to the house along with air and light. The empty spaces are as important as the boundaries that define them. A space is an open invitation for "ten thousand things."

91

Your mind is the same way. The thoughts you think create vessels of belief. The empty space within thoughts is an attracting power to make those thoughts tangible in your life. William Blake wrote, "anything capable of being believed is an image of truth."[2] In this sense, truths are the realities of our three-dimensional world. What we believe becomes an image, an open invitation, for reality.

Charles Kettering once bet an associate that if he had a bird cage in his living room, he'd have to get a bird to go in it. His friend, in good fun, accepted the bet and put a bird cage in his living room. Everyone who came to visit would ask, "What happened to the bird?" Did the bird die?" "Did the bird fly away?" "Where's the bird?" He received so much inquiry and heard so much conversation about the absent bird that he did eventually feel that he had to put a bird in the cage. Kettering won the bet and made his point: when you create a condition in your life—a receptivity for an answer—you will eventually have to get the answer.

An old proverb says, "If you keep a green bough in your heart, the singing bird will come." As you create the receptivity within yourself, you have created a powerful, drawing activity to bring the answers that you want. What you have believed becomes an image to produce a truth—or tangible reality.

Start-Think! Life IS lived from the inside out. As you have the right attitude, life becomes beautiful for you. You can utilize the law of substitution as a means of controlling your thoughts. Change your thoughts to change your head and you change your life. Shift your awareness from one thing to something else. It works!

The same technique also applies to a much deeper level of intensity where you accomplish even more. Your mind shapes your attitude and certainly that shapes the way you look at things. But your outlook also shapes the outcome. More than your experience, your thinking changes reality—it shapes your truths.

There is constant interchange of energies between the viewer and the viewed. We see what is "out there in the world." What we see is determined by what we are prepared to see. Conversely, the "out there" has probably influenced the way we look. Our environment affects us, even as we are constantly influencing our environment. Thinking is the formative power of the universe. The energy is back and forth. Can you see it? Your mind is actually shaping your world.

There are limits, of course. If I think: "tree," I don't become one. Most of us don't directly affect the things around us with thought alone. Perhaps it is because we don't think we can. Jesus was capable of changing conditions, weather, people, even trees by thought alone. Our limits are in our own heads. However, even at the level of belief most of us have achieved, we do not see a direct relationship between our thoughts and surroundings. Let us look more closely.

The absolute Reality of the universe, spelled with a capital "R," is the unalterable nature of God. That Reality is constant. Yet "reality" to each of us personally is many and varied. We live within a "plurality of realities." Two people can look at the same situation and see entirely different things. You can look today and see something else again from what you saw yesterday. Our personal realities are shaped by the turn of our heads (what we *think* is out there). What we envision also, in rough fashion, influences the "out there." We shape our realities and our realities shape us.

A few years ago I discovered an incredible book by the title *The Crack In The Cosmic Egg*.[3] It is a profound, intellectual and metaphysical book written by Joseph Pearce. He proposes that our systems of logic and our sense of values are like eggs because they are closed systems that serve us. Our values are vital and important; they establish a sense of reason out of the otherwise chaos of existence. However, these same systems that we create can also suffocate us. In certain cases, our belief systems become stifling unless we find a way through them. We don't want to shatter the egg and start all over again. We need to find a crack in the egg; to keep our systems intact and to find something beyond the system. Beyond our current reality we can look for and find another reality.

When we perceive a new reality in our minds, it becomes more tangible because of our seeing it. That empty bird cage will draw a bird! The green bough will draw its own. Pearce suggests that science has a way of thinking in terms of "empty categories."[4] Results are shaped by empty categories. Such empty categories are not passive pipe dreams, but rather an active, shaping force to change events. Jesus said that if we had even the faith of a size of a grain of mustard seed, we could say to any mountain, "Be removed," and it would be accomplished (Mark 11:23).

In the same way, the world around us is not always composed of things waiting to be found. Rather, there are things that we ourselves have created. Once we create the vesssel, once we create the branch, once we create a system to support a concept, then we create the object in our world. We build a "new truth" by thinking in terms of a new category. Any new possibility becomes a crack in the egg—a new way of life, a separate reality.

Our thought, in other words, is like a bait of a lure that draws to that category the answer that we believe in. Our thoughts are powerful. When we think into new categories of prosperity regardless of economics, of love in spite of a situation, of feeling healthy in spite of a medical prognosis, we are constructing our own existence.

What the mind believes in, it actually creates. A good example of this fact, demonstrated through hypnosis, is reported by Andrew Weil in his *The Natural Mind:*

> If a subject in good trance is touched by a finger repre-sented to him as a piece of hot metal, an authentic blister will develop at the point of contact. The blister is real. It is produced by autonomic innervation of superficial blood vessels. Obviously there must be an unexplored channel between mind and body, one that is wide open whenever we are in an altered state of consciousness.[5]

The mind can also prevent blisters and pain. Great faith has enabled people to endure incredible situations without ill effects.

Pearce reports that for centuries, in a certain locality in India, a fertility rite was staged. One person was chosen to be the victim of sacrifice to their god to insure the success of the newly planted fields. The victim was prepared with prayer and ceremony. Hooks were placed in the victim's back and tied to a pole secured to an oxcart, which was drawn through the fields, while his body was swung in great arcs over the fields. It was believed that the body, dripping blood over the fields, would insure success to the crops.

About 2000 years ago one such victim did not die. Not only that, but when the hooks were removed, no blood flowed; the wounds healed instantly, and there was no scar. Once it was discovered that the rite could be staged without pain or injury, it has been continuing that way ever since. Evidently, it is still done today. Every year a victim is selected and goes through an initiation of his mind. The preparation in belief prevents him from being harmed. Photographs in *Scientific American*[6] show one such victim who sheds no blood; the wounds have healed immediately, and the man looks happy.

William Blake wrote about a man who did not believe in miracles and thereby made it certain that he would never take part in one. If you do not believe in miracles, then you cannot ever have one. The hardness of heart, the closing-off of the egg, the closing of belief in alternate realities makes it impossible to find new answers. Where your mind goes, power flows.

Charles Fillmore, in his book *Keep a True Lent,* says, "It is the nature of mind to think; your every thought, no matter how trivial, causes vibrations in the universal ether that ultimate in the forms of visibility. You know that the working power of mind is thought and that through thought all conditions that seem to encompass you were formed."[7] All conditions are formed from thoughts. Every thought, no matter how inconsequential, causes a vibration in the mental energy of the universe.

Some of the thoughts flitting through your mind obviously do not stir up much energy. They don't cause many vibrations—they are just flitting through. But, when you concentrate on an idea, and really believe in it as a possibility, then you are creating more power. You are then creating a powerful cage that will capture its own bird. You are creating a powerful binding of a truth.

In the *Atlantic Monthly*[8] magazine was a feature article by Leonard Feinberg on fire-walking in Ceylon (Pearce talks about it in his book). In Ceylon this annual affair is in the honor of the god Kataragama. Three months of initiation are involved in the preparation of this event. After fasting, special diet, ceremonies, prayers and meditation the worshippers are ready. It takes weeks for the big pits of coal to get hot enough so that a piece of paper, wadded up and thrown into the fire, ignites before it touches the coal. At the time of this article, eighty people were participating. Sixty-eight walked on the coals, unharmed; twelve failed. Sixty-eight men and women danced in the coals, walked in the coals, picked them up with their hands and put them over their heads, and were not burned. How is this possible? Fire burns; we know it. They found a crack in the egg. They believed a new reality and it was created.

National Geographic reported another experience with the Ceylon fire walkers. This article, with pictures, was by Gilbert M. Grosvenor, Senior Assistant Editor of *National Geographic,* and his wife. This time the prime participant was a man named Mohotty; he passed steel skewers through another man's cheeks without any blood, without any harm, without any pain. Mohotty, himself, walked on the coals four times at heat measured to be $1,328°$ F.—hot enough to melt aluminum. He also had hooks placed in his back from which he pulled a heavy cart while wearing spiked sandals—the spikes pressing against his bare feet. The hooks were removed: no blood, no pain, no evidence of the hooks. For sixteen years he had continued this ordeal once a year as a religious commitment. Grosvenor asked him his secret and his reply was, "Faith, total faith in my gods."[9]

Faith produced an intense belief that these things were possible. Fire burns! Most of us know that from our own experience. But fire does not always have to burn a particular person, in a particular time, in a particular situation. We also know that a finger touching your arm does not cause a blister; but, as we have seen, it can when the belief is there. Wounds hurt, but they obviously do not always have to hurt. Neither does cancer always have to kill. Neither does a heart condition always have to cripple. Neither do any of the other problems that confront humanity have to be as disastrous as we have believed in the past.

Every experience begins with a thought. The idea is always the beginning of a result. Holding an idea in mind, constantly, is the activity of producing the energy that brings about an answer. Keep your mind focused on a goal, on an objective, on the miracle that you need. *Where attention goes, power flows!* Keep your mind centered on your goal and you must have your results.

Joseph Pearce says there is an observable pattern of creating new realities:

> There is the conscious *desire* for the experience, the asking of the question. There is the *detachment* from the commonplace; the *commitment* to replace the conventional with a new construct; the *passion and decorum*—the

intensive preparation, the gathering of materials for the answer; the *freedom to be dominated* by the subject of desire—the sudden seizure, the breakthrough of mind that gives the inexplicable conviction that it can, after all, be done; and then the *serving* of the new construct, the instant application.[10]

In other words, the secret of experiencing a new reality is the total belief in it—total belief that is constant.

A profound example is that of Joseph Pearce's wife. She had had two massive, radical surgeries for cancer. Malignancy was surging through her. She was given no more than two weeks to live. The evidence was in favor of the terminal verdict. Pearce says:

Nevertheless, I remembered that strange world in which fire could not burn, and entered into a crash program to find that crack in the egg that we might restructure events more in our favor. During five-and six-day fasts, I subjected her to a total "brainwash" day and night, never letting her mind alone. Through all her waking hours I read her literature related to healing, and while she slept I endlessly repeated suggestions of hope and strength. I had no thought of how the restructuring would take place, but in a few hours, some three weeks later she was suddenly healed and quite well.[11]

Constant, intense belief created a new reality. *Start-Think!* The power of mind manifests what it believes. The space in your thought will be filled. Your open invitation must be answered!

In voodoo, when a man learns that he is marked to die, he tends to fulfill that destiny. The same activity occurs in our lives. If we are told that a certain number of us is destined to die from some disease, we hurry to fill the quota.[12] What we need is a new category. We need new, bold beliefs in health; in faith, in riches, in joy! Then we too can walk out on the waves and not sink. As we totally believe in a new category of good, and structure our minds to support that belief, we too can walk on fire and not be burned.

Start-Think! It has not yet appeared—we read in Scriptures—what we shall be.[13] What we shall become is determined by our own determination of what it will be. Issue the open invitation that lures the filling of your new mental categories.

Reality, as we know it, is *organic*! It is living and shapable. So are you. The empty vessels of your thought create a space which the universe is invited to fulfill. Issue these open invitations:

"I know what to do and I do it."

"I can, I can, I can."

"I expect to be healthy and I am."

"I am healed, I am healed, I am healed."

"There is always abundance, and it is mine."

"I am radiant joy in action."

"I enjoy deep and lasting friendships."

"I am a billion brain-celled genius."

"I sizzle with enthusiasm and energy."

Nurture the good that you seek. People do walk on fire and are not hurt. Man has endured wounds without pain. Disease has been healed. You can be healed. You can build a new life. You can get beyond the tragedy of the current divorce; you can do what you need to do and build what you need to build. Don't settle for anything less!

Hang up an empty bird cage. It may not appear that a

bird is anywhere around, but empty categories and empty bird cages do not stay empty for long. According to your faith it is done unto you. You shall say unto this mountain, "Be ye removed," and it shall be!

Start-Think! It is all in your head! Life can be beautiful, sure, if you change your attitude. Life can be even more beautiful as you restructure your thoughts to create the realities you want. Reaffirm your new categories consistently and intently, and as assuredly as two plus two equal four, you will produce a new reality. Every unfilled category is the beginning of a truth. First, you have to create it.

See life as a beautiful experience, free of sickness. You can heal the common cold; get rid of an allergy; cure a terminal disease. You can change your economics. You can issue an invitation to love that must be fulfilled. First, you must think it can be done. Consistently think it possible.

Change your life by changing your head! Commit yourself totally, unequivocally to the category that you want to see filled in your life. Consistently build that bird cage, that branch, that open invitation which will bind on earth the good that you desire. It will be a night and day process. If it's an intense need, then you will intensely respond to it. Say, "I am healed, I am healed, I am healed, I am healed, I am healed!" Say it until your body knows it; until you are healed! Say "I am in tune with the abundant Spirit of God. I am prospered; I am rich, I am rich, I am rich, I am rich!" Say it a thousand, billion, trillion times until the invitation is filled!

Repeated energy produces a non-ambiguous commitment. As you create a category you are going to find proof to support it. You create a belief system, and the energy of the universe will fill it. If you say unto this mountain, "Be ye removed," *and doubt not,* it shall be removed! Issue the invitation! Open the category!

The mountain can be removed. The coals can be walked on. The pain need not affect you. The one-out-of-so-many quota need not be your reality. Totally believe in your good. Begin "to think"—think consistently and intently in the direction of that good. The organic nature of the universe rushes to fill your decree. The lure of the empty category works! Issue the open invitation.

CHAPTER ELEVEN

Health: A Process of Identity

The Life You Seek Is Already Seeking You

One of O. Henry's moving short stories was about a very sick girl who watched the leaves fall from the vine that was clinging to a wall outside her window. In her discouragement, she became convinced that when the last leaf dropped, she would die. Her condition kept getting worse with each falling leaf. Then one night while she slept, an artist friend painted that last leaf on the wall. From the distance, she could not tell that the leaf was painted and it became a symbol of life to her. She recovered and O. Henry had beautifully reinforced an ancient truth: attitude has profound bearing on health.[1]

In 400 B.C., Plato wrote, "We do not cure the body with the body; we cure the body with the mind; and if the mind is confused and upset, it cannot cure anything properly."[2] In *Proverbs* we read, ". . . as he thinketh in his heart, so is he." (Proverbs 23:7) Martin Luther is credited to have said in the sixteenth century, "Heavy thoughts bring on physical maladies. When the soul is oppressed, so is the body."

103

In a simple short story and from the writings of the past we see a clear line of thought that we, ourselves, have something to do with our own health. We all have known that embarrassment can cause a blush; fear can cause our hands to perspire and our mouths to go dry. Quite recently we have been informed how headaches and ulcers are self-imposed. Obviously, what is going on inside our heads influences our health. We call it *psychosomatics*. That means that we, as personalities, have a great deal to do with our own state of health. As we can accept this in some areas, without blame or self-condemnation, we can accept this same responsibility for all our health.

Dr. Henry Huber, M. D., said in a newspaper article:

Before I take a cast off a broken leg I always warn a patient that he is going to find it difficult and painful to start walking again. I have found that the best way to underline the problem is to ask one question: "Who is the only person who can make you walk as well as you did before the accident?" When the patient realizes that he himself must be responsible, he has made a good start toward recovery.[3]

The Will To Live by Dr. Arnold Hutschnecker has become a best-seller. In it he says, "Tiredness without exertion is one of the signs that energies are being used up in an inner struggle between self-destruction and the will to live."[4] He emphasizes repeatedly that this will to live can be directed unconsciously or consciously. He continues, "Illness is an unconscious temporary surrender of the will to live, and repeated illness is a form of slow suicide." Such a statement is strong and true!

We can see the causal power of attitude on our bodies in some illness. Other types of sickness seem to be like nightmares, coming to us without any justification. However, we must accept the responsibility for our total experience in health before we will start doing anything to improve it. Once we see that we have something to do with the sickness, then we will assert the power for greater health.

Howard and Martha Lewis have done incredible research for their book *Psychosomatics*.[5] They trace the complex causes of many diseases, including cancer. Today, because of early detection and numerous physical and mental therapies, more people recover from this dread disease than die from it. We all need to know that! However, we also need to know more of our own responsibility for health. I heard Dr. Carl Simonton speak in Seattle, Washington.[6] He said that healing cancer is easy—the hard part is giving people a reason to live. Much of a healing process is giving the patient a purpose to keep on going. His work in cancer therapy has led him to believe with conviction that sickness is caused and so is health. He says that cancer is frequently a delayed reaction to profound emotional loss. He is proving that group therapy, meditation, and modern medicine can quicken the will to live and produce health.

Dr. Ian Stevenson, psychiatrist and teacher, wrote in *Harper's*, "Recent work has demonstrated the great significance of emotional factors in heart failure and diabetes. Indeed there now remains no organ of the body in which physical changes related to emotions have not been proved of major importance."[7] Dr. William Menninger said simply in *Newsweek*, "Today all diseases are psychosomatic. We have to treat the man, not pieces and parts."[8] Clearly, it's *all* in our heads. We bear the responsibility for our own health. This responsibility is not blame. Blame is a form of self-pity which doesn't help the healing at all. It is a harsh truth, but before we do something about our health we need to accept responsibility for our whole selves.

Responsibility invokes action. Something must be done and can be done. We can keep open categories of health in our minds. It is up to us to believe so totally in health that our will to live is quickened and renewed daily. To accept responsibility is to be willing to work on health. "Ye shall know the truth and the truth shall make you free." (John 8:32) By changing our heads we can change our health. Paul writes, "Be renewed in the spirit of your mind." (Ephesians 4:23) To affirm health is to reveal health. I believe it was Dr. Sara Jordon who said clearly, "The simple cure of many states of disability is to give your mind a good shampoo every day." Get inside your head with ideas of health. Paint the leaf on the wall, shampoo the inside of your head, renew your consciousness to health. Take action!

Your role in healing is not purely passive! Revive Coue's motto, "Every day in every way I am getting better and better." It might be an empty category—but as you fill it with the energy of your faith it will lure the answer you seek. You have created your disease; you can also create your health. Make up your mind you want to be healthy. Talk up to yourself about health. One man said, "Every time we speak we cause the atoms of our body to tremble and change their places."[9] Your own words can cause your body to sing and dance into life.

The reality of health is organic. You shape your own experiences in health and vitality. You have all you need to be healthy; health is actually seeking you, and your own words and actions can shape your body to identify with more health. That which you are seeking is already seeking you! Your wholeness is the *Reality* within your experienced *reality*. Health is yours!

Eric Butterworth says in his book *Unity of All Life:*

> Anything less than wholeness in the body gives evidence of a "frustration of potentiality," a concealment of the whole person. There is that in you that is whole though your body may be racked with pain. There is that in you that is whole though you may be trapped in some form of addiction. The whole of you is the reality of you, the God-self of you. No matter how partial may be the experience of wholeness in the body, the you that is more than a body is still whole . . . you can be healed because there is always an allness within your illness.[10]

The health you seek is already seeking you. The whole of the tree is within the seed. The wholeness of the bird is contained within the egg. The Reality of God is trapped within you and can be released. Butterworth quotes Edmund Sinnott: "There must be present in a plant living stuff . . . something that represents the natural configuration of the whole . . ."[11] The intelligence of God is always more than the substance of God—even while both are eternally present. The intelligence that holds molecules together transcends those particles. I heard Dr. Elmer Green say it this way, "All of the body is in the mind but not all of the mind is in the body."[12] Your mind is more than your body and can make you well. Your mind contains the pattern of wholeness; "there is an allness within your illness."

Prayerful affirmations and silent meditations change us so that more of the Reality of wholeness is seen. In this sense, we do not make health but rather reveal the health that is already there. When we experience sickness, we are not conforming to the intelligence of God. When we experience health, we are cooperating with Universal Intelligence. In a strict sense, we are not shaping a new reality but revealing that Reality which was there all the time. Health is the Reality and it is seeking you! God is there already. Allness is there already. To know this is to prove it.

"For we know in part, and we prophesy in part. But when that which is perfect is come, then that which is in part shall be done away." (I Corinthians 13:9–10) We often see the parts. When we see the all, it asserts itself. Confront the bigger Reality and it becomes your experienced reality. Identify with wholeness!

In Bangkok there is a famous Buddha.[13] For many years this ten-foot-high, eight-ton cement statue stood in a temple courtyard. No one knew its history. When the temple was renovated in 1955, the priest decided to move the Buddha inside. On a given day, a large crane came to do the moving. When the sculpture was two feet off the ground, the rope broke and the heavy statue crashed to the ground. It didn't shatter, but an ugly crack appeared across its front. Then a heavy rain began so work was called off for that day.

The next morning, the priest went to look at the Buddha. Through the crack he thought he saw light. He walked closer. The rain had soaked in, causing some of the plaster to fall out. What appeared first as light, was seen, on closer inspection, to be gold! With his bare hands, the priest was able to pull away more of the plaster and expose more gold. When all the concrete was removed, there was revealed a five-and-a-half ton gold Buddha—the world's largest chunk of solid gold!

Now the earlier history is known. It was created in 1255 A.D. by order of the King of Siam. To protect the golden Buddha from approaching enemies, the village people of the time coated it with the concrete. The secret had been lost, but the gold was there all the time. The outer grey was all that could be seen, but the greater splendor was inside all along.

In our lives we often see only the concrete. We see in part. The allness is there. When we see it, "that which is in part shall be done away." Gold is within YOU! God is within you! Health is the Reality of you. See the gold, see the power within the seed, see God in your flesh. Make that move in your own head that identifies with health. The splendor is there. *Start-Think!* See health with your mind through an empty category and Reality is your reality!

This process of identification reveals greater health. Direct all your faith toward that wholeness you seek. Realize for yourself, *"I am a process of identity in a universe of potentiality."*[14] Affirm that for yourself! Health is a process of claiming the splendor of God— your potential of life. As you identify with your potential you unfold increasing degrees of health and vitality.

The process of identification with allness is always forward. You can never go backward. If you lived in a dark cellar and thought that was all there was, you would make the most of it. When you discover that the entire house is there and it is yours, you will never again confine yourself to the cellar.[15] As you proceed to realize the health that is wanting to express through you, you will never be content to stay in sickness. To see the cosmos is to move into consciousness beyond the microcosmic. The parts can no longer hold you. You have, with Emerson, contemplated the facts of life from the highest point of view. Such an identification permanently changes you.

Here is the secret of affirmation. When you speak words of health with conviction you are identifying with the All. The seed is there. The gold is already within. Your affirmations are the empty categories that bring forth that which is really you. You can affirm, "God is my health, I can't be sick," and know you are releasing the hidden splendor of health that is within you. When you say, "I am radiant, vibrant, eternal life," you are seeing "that which is perfect is come" and the limitation can no longer confine you. Any condition can reveal a part of you. Affirm, "God is the All of me and He is now revealed through me." Truly start "to think"! The increased life you are seeking is seeking you! Lay hold of new health by affirming ideas such as these:

"I am healed, healed, healed!"

"My body is a perfect expression of the One."

"I shampoo my mind every day with the truth that Health is my Reality."

"My experience in health comes through my process of identification with health."

"The category of radiant health is now filled to over-flowing in me."

"My reality is God's Reality of infinite wholeness."

"I am healthy now and I shall stay that way."

Combine your affirmations of health with visualizations of the healing activity. I have on my desk a remarkable photograph taken by the renowned medical photographer Lennart Nilsson.[16] It shows white blood cells defending against bacteria in the bloodstream. It is one of several Nilsson photos designed to create never-before-seen portraits of the human body. The white blood cells look like small spheres massed before a nebulous shape on a turbulent sea. Picture it in your head. Ping-pong balls attacking and devouring an enemy bacteria. How incredible to be able to see this daily drama within our bodies! Such a picture is a powerful visualization to reveal more of the health within.

A vivid imagination is a valuable help in healing. As you mentally see the category you would have filled, you give power to that direction. Your imagination can also "see" the process of healing. Visualize those white blood cells devouring the enemy. Strengthen their natural activity by "cheering" them on with your thoughts. Speak an affirmation. Can you see what is happening? You are creating a reality from the Reality of God. See yourself vital, whole, healthy! See the process! "Watch" the cells build themselves; the white cells purifying your system. Continue to think and speak affirmations. In this context, you are using your imagination in three ways, (1) to define a direction of health, (2) to picture the end result, and (3) to picture the process of your body accomplishing this goal. When your imagination is working for you in this three-fold manner, you will find your faith is augmented and your affirmations have increased power to help bring forth your healing.

When you combine your affirmations with powerful,

mental pictures, you are getting your entire head going in one direction. In fact, affirmations work best when you picture creative images. Such an image may be symbolic or factual. Here is actually a fourth way to use your imagination for healing. In addition to the other images which are directly related to your affirmation, you may find it helpful to associate something symbolic which represents health to you. As you affirm health, you can also see a baby laughing, a bird in flight, a flower blooming, a tree growing tall and straight, a light growing brighter. Pick a symbol that represents healing to you; one may emerge out of your own consciousness without conscious effort.

Have you ever heard of a "totem?" Many ancient tribes had one animal or plant that was held sacred. Such was their totem. Modern psychology sometimes refers to that same tendency within individuals, usually in their childhood. A particular tree, a dog, a horse, or anything may become symbolic to the individual, often emerging in dreams. If such a "totem" is now a part of your consciousness or you can remember it being so, that can be a powerful symbolic visualization to picture during your affirmations. This technique can be valuable for all types of demonstration in addition to healing. Don't force it; if it happens, use it for your advantage. If you don't identify with such a totem image, that is fine, let it go.

Now then, let's create a discipline using these techniques. *Stop-Think-Start!* Give yourself time to really stop. Breathe deeply; consciously relax for three to five minutes. Think quiet thoughts and visualize your body letting go of all tension. After this stop, think into the direction of healing you desire. Speak an affirmation such as "I am healed, healed, healed!" Now visualize the specific experience of health you desire, and speak the affirmation again. Breathe deeply several times. Now visualize yourself as if you were already experiencing the category of health you have chosen. Holding that picture, speak your affirmation again, "I am healed, healed, healed!" Let your mind flow gently—relax.

Next picture the cells of your body creating the new health—"see" the white blood cells defending against the bacteria. Speak your affirmation with this image in mind. Be still. If you are comfortable with a symbol and it seems natural to you, select or allow a symbolic image to enter your awareness. Perhaps the light, the tree, the flower is your totem or you will make it so. With your symbolic totem in mind, speak your affirmation, "I am healed, healed, healed!" Let go. Open your eyes, or continue to repeat the entire exercise. Choose to dwell on any part of the exercise that appeals to you. You are totally involved in the category of health. That health is seeking you. Your *Start-Think!* is opening the door to reveal the golden splendor. Your cells are trembling and changing their places!

After a meeting I once held in Hilo, Hawaii, a woman in the audience shared this story with everyone there. Since her own children are grown, she has spent much time teaching ideas and affirmations to her neighbor boy, with the blessing of his parents. He is seven years old. One morning, while his mother was out, he reached across a hot stove. His pajamas caught fire and he was badly burned. He was rushed to the hospital and arrived semi-conscious; his eyes were closed. To determine how conscious the boy was, the doctor asked, "Do you know who you are?"

A weak voice answered groggily, through the pain, "I am a healthy, happy child of God." His healing was rapid and complete! The discipline of affirmations had paid off. He knew who he was! Even half-conscious he identified with health and that Reality filled his being.

Health is within YOU! You can be healthier than ever before. Visualize images of health and speak affirmations of health at the same time. It is up to you to keep that last leaf on the wall—to take responsibility for your own healing. The will to live responds to your demand. All diseases are psychosomatic; so are all experiences in healing. Shampoo your mind daily to cause the atoms of your body to tremble with vitality. The life you seek is already seeking you. "There is always an allness within your illness." As you see the gold, the limitations drop away. You are "a process of identity in a universe of potentiality." Affirm life. Use your imagination to define your health, picture your results, strengthen the process of health, and to symbolize God's wholeness within you. With your inner vision and your words you are luring the infilling of your category of health. *Start-Think!* Health is a process of identification!

PART FIVE

Stop—Think—Start!
The Ultimate Objective

CHAPTER TWELVE

Don't Think about Hippopotamus

Think About God!

We have been dealing with *Stop-Think-Start!* on two basic levels: (1) Comfort and (2) Demonstration. By thinking in terms of that which is pleasant rather than upsetting, we can feel better about our lives, be less neurotic, experience more happiness. That is certainly *comfortable.* We can *Stop-Think-Start!* into dynamics of faith and imagination and create greater results. We can change our everyday realities into more health, prosperity, and joy. To *demonstrate* results is certainly a practical use of our minds.

However, an even higher level of application is to stop trying to "get something" and open ourselves to "be someone." Now we shall consider the use of spiritual words, balance them with silence, enter into meditation, and open our awareness to all life. First of all, don't think about hippopotamus!

When I say to you, "Don't think about hippopotamus," you may well reply, "I'm not—at least I wasn't until you suggested the idea." Now you *are* thinking about hippopotamus. You might even go so far as to try "not-to-think," which is almost the same thing. Either way you are thinking about that which I asked you not to think.

Walter Pitkin said the secret of absolute power is, "Never think . . . of the word *hippopotamus*."[1] Anyone who can control his head in such a way as to turn off an unwanted thought at will can do anything. *Stop-Think!* You don't have to think about something undesired. You can "not think" about anything!

However, once a thought enters the field of your awareness, and you try to forget it or put it out of your mind, it persistently claims your attention. Consequently, Pitkin says that if you could learn how *not* to think about *hippopotamus,* even for an instant, it would mean that you had gained a marvelous power over your mind.

When was the last time you tried "not-to-think" about a problem or concern? You wanted to go to sleep, be happy, enjoy the party, or be free of worry. Your mind was obsessed with a "hippopotamus" of a problem—illness, lack of money, real or imagined difficulties. You may have told yourself not to worry. Yet you kept right on. The more you tried "not-to-think" about something the more it claimed your attention.

Have you ever tried to lose something on purpose? It can't be done. You have misplaced items and you have forgotten where you last saw something. That was when you were not paying attention. If you put your glasses on the bookcase and say to yourself, "Now I am going to lose these glasses and forget I put them on the bookcase," you will remember easily where you put them.

When you give conscious energy to something, you reinforce it. Similarly, you can't deliberately set out to "not worry" without giving it more attention. Then you are worried. You are thinking about a "hippopotamus" again.

There is a way of "not thinking" about hippopotamus or anything else about which you would prefer "not-to-think." Remember from the law of substitution that your mind can go in only one direction at a time. You can turn your mind most effectively from one subject to another by concentrating on the other subject. This is the secret of absolute power: think about something else!

What is it you don't want to think about? Face it with a confrontive denial. Say to yourself, "I won't think about this." Then don't think about it; think about something else. It is no use to keep repeating what you won't do—you only reinforce the undesired thought that way. *Decide what you are going to do and do it!* I have a poster which I enjoy. It says in large, fancy letters, "Repent and be saved." Then in small print below, it says, "In case you have already repented, kindly disregard this notice."[2] Once you have turned your mind away from something undesired, then keep going forward. Don't keep repenting—concentrate on what you want.

The ultimate objective of redirecting your mind is to think about God. You have already applied many levels of *Stop-Think-Start!* and found that they work. Any substitution that improves your outlook is a step forward. Now apply the technique to scientific prayer—*think about God!* Emmet Fox says this is the Golden Key to harmony and happiness. All you do is this: *"Stop thinking about the difficulty, whatever it is, and think about God instead.* This is the complete rule, and if only you will do this, the trouble, whatever it is, will presently disappear. It makes no difference what kind of trouble it is . . . just stop thinking about it, and think of God instead—that is all you have to do."[3]

Stop thinking about the "hippopotamus" of a situation and turn your attention to God. Your head can go only one way at a time. When you contemplate God for even a few minutes you are not thinking about a problem.

What do you think about when you think of God? When you think about God, you are usually thinking about that part of the Infinite that represents "God" to you. God Himself is the open category beyond all others. He becomes to you very much as you see Him. The nature of the Absolute is incomprehensible in total. Yet, your experience with the Absolute becomes what you are prepared to see. The intelligent-energy that is God is the essence of everything. God is all and all is God. Whatever way you see God, is God to you.

Anything you substitute is also part of God. When you think about your thought processes, that is part of God. When you confront your fears and talk to yourself about them, that is God. When you practice positive thinking, think about pleasant activities, get busy physically, that too is God. When you couple your faith and imagination into empty categories of good, that is God. Your every thought is one of God. Choose which thought helps you the most!

You do not play the game of golf with only one club. You have at least four woods and five irons to use for different situations. So it is with the game of thinking.

You have various techniques and skills to use, depending on what you have to do and what seems to work best in a given situation. Use all your clubs! Use all the techniques of *Stop-Think-Start!* and realize that one way or another you can control your head.

In this light, every *Stop-Think-Start!* is a prayer. Prayer isn't limited to religious words; everything you've read in this book is a type of prayer. Anything you do to move your head to a better perspective is a prayer. However, when your words and mental images are more closely approximating the Absolute, you have directed your awareness to a "higher degree" of prayer. When you reach that level of actually thinking about God, you have shifted into the ultimate dimension of prayer.

In a health-need situation, you might experience the gamut of prayer like this: you would think about something pleasant instead of your pain. A positive situation will make you feel better and ultimately help in the healing. Yet, you strike a higher octave of prayer when your substitution is to thoughts of health. To think and speak in terms of more life will open new categories. Then move into an even higher dynamic of prayer and think in terms of God-as-health. Your affirmations get closer to the absolute experience of prayer as you mentally and verbally attach your objective to God. Finally transcend even the category you would see expanded to think in terms of the Absolute. Each step is a degree of awareness in which you have increased your conscious identity with God.

While the word "prayer" is usually applied only to spiritual words, any thought that moves you forward is truly a prayer and should be used. However, the highest degree of prayer is to actually think about God. Do it! Consciously think about God in God-like terms. Identify with the Infinite. Pray in words that consciously connect you to God.

All problems begin in the mind and are supported by the mind. The bondage is all in your head. That's where the freedom is too. Take your mind off the "hippopotamuses" and put it on God. Your mind grows on what it is fed; feed it on God. Speak words of God. Continue in those words and be free indeed. "Every word has within it the power to make manifest whatever man decrees, but especially spiritual words have this power."[4]

Affirm spiritual words, such as:

"There is no power but God."

"God is with me."

"I believe! I believe! I believe!"

"I am now open to God's good in my life."

"Nothing but good can happen to me for God is all there is."

Memorize Bible passages that create a continuity of spiritual words, such as:

"The Lord is my shepherd; I shall not want." (Ps. 23:1)

"Fear thou not; for I am with thee." (Isa. 41:10)

"In all thy ways acknowledge him, and he shall direct thy paths." (Pro. 3:6)

"Thou wilt keep him in perfect peace, whose mind is stayed on thee." (Isa. 26:3)

"Ask and it shall be given you; seek, and ye shall find; knock, and it shall be opened unto you." (Mt. 7:7)

Don't think about hippopotamus. Think about God. Don't think about the problem—think about the answer: God. Keep knowing the truth of God's presence and power, and you shall be free from what was disturbing you.

When you repeat such ideas over and over you give them more power. Repetition fixes a word in your mind. You direct more energy when you give your good greater attention. Think about God; speak words of God. Your words can energize your body with greater health. Your words can bless your world. You can speak words of prosperity, can feel rich ideas sparking your mind. Get your mind repeatedly on the truth of God. Continue in words of God. *"Continue in my word . . . and the truth shall make you free."*

Recently I received a letter from a young lady who is a member of a congregation I formerly served. Her letter tells about her career, her friends, and her plans. She enclosed a newspaper interview with pictures that told about her successful life-style. (I'll call her Laurie, which isn't her real name.) Her life is certainly going well. It wasn't always so.

The first time I heard of Laurie was when she called me at home late at night. She was on the verge of suicide. The man with whom she was living had left her, her job was folding, and nothing seemed to be going right. We talked for a long time and she promised to meet me in the morning. She had only heard of these ideas through a friend and knew nothing about directing her own mind and her own life. When we met the following morning she did most of the talking; I only listened. Eventually, I was able to reflect some of her statements back to her so that she began to see how she was not only setting herself up for much of her unhappiness but was compounding situations by her inner dialogue.

Laurie began attending church and classes, reading everything I gave her. There were serious setbacks during the months that followed, but there was constant progress. She faced her problems so she no longer had to run from them. She took responsibility for her own head and disciplined her thinking. She began to repeatedly speak spiritual words. Now, every day she continues to prove to herself that life can be beautiful. With her head going forward, her life is going forward as well. She is a living example of Jesus' words, *"Let not your heart be troubled . . . believe in God . . . "* (John 14:1)

Another example is a husband and wife I shall call Jack and Marge (not their real names). The main issue was Jack's drinking—which he wouldn't admit. He had drunk himself into oblivion every evening. Now he was starting with breakfast. He was vicious with the children, had just beaten Marge, and his previously successful sales career was slipping badly. I met with Jack and Marge together and with each of them separately. Jack continually refused to face his problem or even admit he had one. He flatly refused help from Alcoholics Anonymous (A. A.). Then he refused even to talk to me.

Marge and I worked without Jack to keep our thoughts on God. Every other day presented a new crisis. Finally, Jack was fired. Their expensive new home had to be sold in a depressed market. We continued to pray. We talked together daily, speaking the word that God was in charge to heal, guide, and prosper.

When the house was sold, Marge moved into a small apartment with one child. The older children moved in with friends, and Jack was nowhere to be seen. The situation was tense, but Marge continued in her faith—

constantly affirming, "God is in charge and God is only good." She continued in her words and kept her consciousness centered on God.

Then, after two weeks, Jack came home. He had attended three A. A. meetings and wanted to come to church with Marge. He was determined he was going to make it—and he did. Jack began praying and meditating regularly. He insisted I be his guest at an A. A. meeting where he was the speaker.

That was five years ago. Now we laugh together about the past. Jack and Marge are happy and more prosperous than ever before. Marge's use of *Stop-Think-Start!* certainly gives evidence to the scripture, *"If ye abide in me, and my words abide in you, ye shall ask what ye will, and it shall be done unto you."* (John 15:7)

Active in another church where I once served is a great guy named Jim. He, his wife, Jill, (not their real names) and their children apply prayer techniques every day. One night I received an emergency telephone call from Jill. Jim was in the intensive-care unit of the city hospital. When I got to his bedside he was only partly conscious. Everything was being done that was possible to keep Jim alive and determine a diagnosis and treatment. Jim weakly nodded that he knew I was there and would pray as best he could. Jim, Jill, and I prayed. We didn't pray long, but we prayed words of healing. We spoke of Jim's body to cooperate with what the doctors were doing and to be quickened into perfect life. The specific words said were not so important as the quality of words to identify with God. We grounded ourselves in thinking about God instead of illness.

At ten o'clock the next morning my telephone rang

again. This time it was Jim. He was fine. No one seemed to know what had been wrong or what had happened, but he was fine. He stayed for another day of observation and then was sent home. In two more days he was back at work and by Sunday was helping me at church. The miraculous power of God is mighty to heal. *Stop-Think-Start!* The ultimate objective is to contact God consciously! *"All things are possible to him that believeth."* (Mark 9:23)

You can be healed! You can be prospered! You can be happy! You can control your own head. Stop thinking about the "hippopotamus," about Aunt Jennifer, the lawyers, the pain. Think about life. Think about abundance. Think about God! *"Ye shall know the truth and the truth shall make you free."*

You can work at directing your head. Over and over again fill your mind with words about God. Yes, God is more than words, but before you go beyond your words, take them as far as they will go. Pray in words that tie you to God. When you fill your mind with God, God fills your life as increased blessings. You can't think about the problem when you are thinking about God. *"Thou shalt forget thy misery, and remember it as waters that pass away."* (Job 11:16) Don't think about hippopotamus or anything else that would intensify your unhappiness. *Stop-Think-Start!* Think about God!

CHAPTER THIRTEEN

An Altogether Other Dimension

Experience More of the Absolute

What is God? What is our Ground of Being, the Absolute, this Ultimate Objective? We say the words and think we know what they mean—but do we? Surely, God is more than words. These printed symbols on a page cannot contain the nature of the Infinite. To experience more of God we have to get beyond our words—take them as far as they will go and then reach farther. As Emerson said so well, "Let a man believe in God, and not in names and places and persons."[1]

Words are not the things they represent; yet, how easily we confuse the two. A horse is not a word spelled h-o-r-s-e. It is a type of animal we have named in English: horse. Likewise, God is more than a three-letter word spelled G-o-d. What is God? We do not want to be like the character in the novel *Pilgrim's Inn* of whom it was said, "His religion had never consisted in more than believing in God without having even asked himself what he meant by God."[2] We want to believe in God that is beyond a word; beyond a name.

Stop-Think-Start! What do you mean when you say "God?" How do you define God? What is the Ultimate,

127

the Ground of Being to you? Ask yourself! How you define the Absolute shapes your relationship with God. What you think about the nature of God influences how you think and pray. The way in which you define *Reality* will mold the *realities* of your experience. Charles Fillmore stated, "The starting point in spiritual realization is a right understanding of the one designated as the almighty."[3] What do you mean by "God"?

Some people have learned in Sunday school about a "grand old man" kind of God—He's old, vindictive, and effective. Yet, He seems more a God of the past. In addition, the concept of God as a long-bearded man living above the clouds doesn't seem to fit with the twentieth-century knowledge we have of our universe. Men have traveled as far as the moon without any confrontation or protest from a God out there in the sky. The concepts of the past no longer are adequate. God is so much more!

Much of the problem is one of semantics. Abstractions are difficult to convey. We almost have to resort to words, images, characterizations. Santa Claus is a grand symbol of the spirit of Christmas which is love, joy and giving. At an early age we question the personality of Santa Claus and discover, "Yes, Virginia, there is a Santa Claus"—but he is different from what we were earlier led to believe. The literal mind of a child sometimes refuses to grasp the transition from symbol to fact. A youngster can demand: "Either there is or isn't!" Yet, we know it isn't that simple. Santa is not a literal person, yet is a real quality within every person who loves and laughs and shares.

So it is with God. The limits of language impose on us a man-like God with human attributes and qualities.

When we outgrow such a God we can also demand: "Either He is or He isn't!" God is! He is so much more than we have thought—bigger than the limiting image we embraced in our innocence.

Whatever you have thought about God, He (She) is yet more. God is not a being, but a beingness itself. Not a spirit, but Spirit, Being, Life itself. Not a mind, but all Mind; all intelligence. Not a man, but the Idea of personhood encompassing all mankind. Not only omnipresent, but Omnipresence. All that is, is God. God is the essence and the expression in all; the Ground of Being and as well the emanations of all Beingness.

In other words, God is the idea of light as well as the light that shines in the darkness. God is even the darkest shadow—remember, there are no opposites. There is only God; there is only light—everywhere present yet expressing in varying degrees. There is no ugliness; there is only some degree of beauty. There is no sickness; there is only life, manifest to some degree of health. God is all—so much more than we have thought.

When we concentrate on the literal images we can fail to go beyond them to the greater dimensions of understanding. Yet, when we reach for newer, larger concepts we still get stuck in cliches, new symbols, different words. How difficult it is to be explicit when dealing with the Absolute. Is it any wonder we gravitate to the child-like images of God-as-person? Our literal minds, the limits of language, the common male pronouns almost force us into speaking of a "God of names and places and persons." We must go further!

God is life—all life! The varying degrees of life in every particle of the universe is God in motion. Truly, "In him we live, move, and have our being." (Acts 17:28)

God is the life that animates you, as personal and meaningful to you as the life you are living. God is love—all love! God is the love that you receive and that you give. God is intelligence—all intelligence! That same wisdom that frames the universe, builds your body; it guides you to the degree you are in tune with it. God is Spirit, Being, Presence, Intelligence, Love, Power, Allness.

On and on go the adjectives and synonyms. They are still only words. God is more. We get closer when we admit a mystery. More than any dogma or definition, God is more! Eventually we come to feel, along with Einstein, that God is the basic mystery and integrity of the universe.[4] Yes, God is a cohesive, intelligent, dynamic mystery—seemingly incomprehensible. Our words falter, yet they keep moving us closer to Truth. Words lead to more words beyond "names and places and persons"—we have taken our words as far as they will go. *Now we must go beyond words.*

"An altogether other dimension" of God is experiencing that presence of the Absolute. God cannot be adequately defined—only inadequately experienced. When we reach the limit of words we are ready to "know" God, which is beyond simply "knowing about" Him. "When we have broken our God of tradition and ceased from our god of rhetoric, then may God fire the heart with his presence," Emerson writes.[5] Now is the time, in the words of Meister Eckhart, to "let God be god in you." Beyond words, as valuable as they are, is the silence where God becomes Himself in us. Like our words, the experience of such silence is never adequate, never complete—but always fulfilling, always healing, ever renewing.

This feeling is captured in Walt Whitman's "The Learn'd Astronomer." He describes sitting in a confining classroom listening to a tedious lecture about the stars until:

> How soon unaccountable I became tired and sick,
> Till rising and gliding out I wander'd off by myself,
> In the mystical moist night-air, and from time to time,
> Look'd up in perfect silence at the stars.[6]

To experience the stars on a quiet night is totally different from talking about them. Beyond our words about God, He "fires the heart with his presence." We can be born into a new dimension of experience as delicious as a starry night. With our words we claim responsibility for our own lives; we can integrate all our energies to go forward. We can comfort our hearts with positive words and open new categories of health, happiness, and riches. Our words take us all the way to God. Then we let go of our words—let go to feel the fire of His presence.

There is an old saying, "You are forever sweeping out the house but you never let go of the broom." As we use our words, we must also let go. Our thinking can only do so much; after that, silence is necessary. The letting-go that follows the word is a silence where the greatest work is accomplished.

Paul Brunton writes in *Discover Yourself:*

> By logical, rational thinking, you may find a human solution, by ceasing to think, by taking no thought and relinquishing your problem, the higher power is then given an opportunity to deal with it. To take no thought means to still the mind; to sit and enter into real meditation. Thereby the Overself is given a chance to come and take thought on your behalf for you.[7]

Silence, following thought and word, opens you to the greater experience.

"Now is the time," says Daniel Yankelovich, "to give the right hemisphere a break." The right side of the brain houses the intuitive aspect of consciousness. Recent studies indicate our logic emerges through the left lobe of the brain while our hunches emerge through the right hemisphere. After we have employed our reason we can enter silent meditation that utilizes the other side of the brain. Now is the time to ". . . open oneself up to the more intuitive side of one's mind, to derigidify the familiar, cognitive style, to leave oneself open to new possibilities, new modes of experience, new modes of perception and consciousness, to hang a little looser . . ."[8] Now is the time to let go of the broom; go beyond our words, taste or feel more of God!

We need to sweep the house; we also need to stop and be still. We have a living to make and a life to live. It's a matter of having a goal and a role, achievement as well as authenticity, efficiency and ecstasy. Only in the quiet that follows our actions can we also be someone, experience who we are, fill a role, be authentic, and feel the ecstasy of God. Both aspects of thinking are necessary; we can have both! We work to accomplish greater good, reach goals, and become efficient. We can also be new beings, one with the light, one with the Absolute, one with the inner ecstasy. Think a greater-than-usual stop! Let go of the broom; be still. Think: *Stop!* A new *Start!*

This is the height of the mystical experience which William James described so well:

> The further limits of our being plunge, it seems to me, into an altogether other dimension of existence from the visible . . . world. Name it the mystical region, or the

> supernatural region, whichever you choose . . . we belong to it in a more visible world . . . When we commune with it, work is actually done upon our finite personality, for we are turned into new men.[9]

There is "an altogether other dimension" of God to be experienced.

Remember the ancient instruction was, "Be still and know . . ."[10] It is a double command: be quiet and be busy. Do your thinking and knowing; then be quiet and let go. As the brain itself has two hemispheres to perform active and passive functions, so are you to actively think and then quietly plunge into "the further limits of your being." Both are modes of consciousness; each has its own standard equipment in your head. Know AND be still; be still AND know.

Thinking functions through these two modes called "active and passive" or "choice and freedom." In many ancient rituals of meditation, a word or mantra is "chosen" to set the mind in a particular direction. Then the mind is "freed" or released to experience that "altogether other dimension of existence." All prayers can function in the same way. Speak a word, an affirmation, a Scripture, or any prayer and do not stop there. Create a quiet space following the mode of choice wherein your consciousness is free.

Life does not exist with only inhales or only exhales. Both are necessary, in alternating patterns. Your consciousness flows in much the same way. Think the thought, sweep the floor. Then let go, release, exhale. Pluck the string of the lyre of your mind; let it sound. Strike the gong; wait for the vibrations to fill all space.

A person's life can be lopsided with too much action

and not enough peace. Likewise, our thinking and our praying are often too many words and not enough "other" of silence. You have heard people "say a prayer" which consists of many words rapidly strung together with special intonation and ending with "amen." You felt nothing. The string had been plucked and dampened at almost the same instant. There was no quiet for the song to fill.

Table blessings are expected to be short. After all, the food is ready and everyone is hungry. The conditions are ripe to "get it over with and eat." Have you noticed how most table blessings are just so many words with some sixteenth-century "thee's" and "thou's" to make them seem religious? Since social gatherings are filled with words anyway, the prayer offers little variation from the rest of the conversation. If you have to leave something out, why not leave out the words? Thirty seconds of silence can much more effectively heal the soul, tie hearts together, and truly give thanks. All prayer includes words; deeper prayer goes further to include silences. The silence can be the most important part.

Prayer and meditation are terms often used interchangeably. To me, meditation is the silence included in prayer. Prayer itself is the aiming of consciousness. It is pursuing, choosing, thinking. Prayer is directing awareness; projecting answers. Meditation, on the other hand, is touching the Source within. It is listening, assimilating, absorbing. Meditation is hearing the sound after the note has been struck. It is watching the wake that follows the ship. In the stillness that follows the "knowing" the work is done.

End every "think" with a "stop." Pause within your

prayers and at their conclusion. Such "stops" always lead to other "thinks." Your prayers and meditations alternate and intertwine like breathing itself. End every "think" with a "stop" and end every "stop" with a "think." Think; stop. Stop; think. Embellish your prayers with more silence. *Stop-Think! Think-Stop! Start-Think! Think-Start!*

Don't think about problems, think about God. Not in blind reaching, without having asked yourself what you mean by "light" or "God." Instead, question your meanings; define your terms. Transcend your symbols to experience more of the mystery and integrity that is God. Speak your affirmations, prayers, and mantras as far as they will go. Then let go of the broom; add enough silence so that God may fire your heart with His presence. The ultimate objective of all thought is to experience more of the Absolute, to follow your prayers with enough silence to plunge yourself into that altogether "other" dimension of feeling God. Now you are ready for the technique that is more "stop" than "think." Stop your thoughts and enter the sound of silence.

CHAPTER FOURTEEN

The Sound of Silence

Plumb Full of Hush to the Brim

Some scientists pay more attention to what you don't say, and how you don't say it, than even your most brilliant utterances. These "pausologists" are studying why man punctuates his speech with pauses and what these pauses mean. Evidently, frequent pauses in speech indicate that new, creative speech is being expressed, while fewer pauses indicate the words have been used before. There are many kinds of pauses, including silent, juncture, hesitation; even pauses filled with "er-r-r, um, ah, uh, and m-m-m" to keep someone else from interrupting. The pausologists estimate that between 40 and 50 percent of spontaneous speech is pause-time, and that these pauses are as important to speech as the spoken word itself.[1] You see, you experience the sounds of silence every day. Your own speech is filled with silence.

In writing, we show our speech silences with punctuation. Even the spaces between the words are necessary, as are the spaces between lines. When you look at a printed page and see how much blank space there actually is, you get an idea of how much "silence" there is in speech. Every silence means something; every silence says something. Listen to the silence!

One of Emily Dickinson's poems begins:

> To hear an oriole sing
> May be a common thing
> Or only a divine

She concludes:

> The tune is in the tree
> The skeptic showeth me
> "No, Sir! In Thee?"[2]

The song is in you and so is the silence. The sound of the bird as beauty or distraction is all in your own head. So is the sound of silence. Think into a listening "stop" that hears more within the silence.

Pythagoras taught his students first of all, "Learn to be silent. Let your quiet mind listen and absorb." A quiet mind is a listening one. Listen to what you can hear in silence. Listen within. Draw into Emerson's "heart of silence." Ram Dass calls it the "heart cave." Here within is a tune of silence, a sound of hush that will teach, guide, inspire, and fulfill. Pause, and listen.

Alone in nature is a silence; your busy ears have forgotten. Taste the quiet of the out-of-doors, alone. Go for a walk in the woods by yourself. Climb a mountain and listen to the quiet. After a few minutes you will hear your own swallowing, noises from your stomach, breathing, a distant pounding and a faint buzz. The pounding is your own pulse and the hissing is the sound of blood moving through your head. These are some of the sounds of silence you might never hear unless you listen. Continue in quiet listening and experience the loudness of your own thoughts. Beyond these sounds is a greater silence and a calm. The voice of God is silence, more like a hush than a tone, yet a sound.

Kahlil Gibran wrote:

> My soul is my counsel and has taught me to give ear to the voices which are created neither by tongues nor uttered by throats. Before my soul became my counsel I was dull and weak of hearing, reflecting only upon the tumult and the cry. But, now, I can listen to silence with serenity and can hear in the silence the hymns of ages chanting exultation to the sky and revealing the secrets of eternity.[3]

The tune of silence is within you; listen!

Most of us seem to have lost the knack for quiet listening, yet it is one of our native abilities. For our ancestors, listening was necessary for survival, for a sound often warned of danger. Today, our lives are vastly different. Our survival often demands that we *not* listen! We are surrounded by many sounds, often of extreme volume. We can keep our sanity only by shutting out the sounds around us. However, in closing out the world, we are closing out the inner silence as well. We need to learn to be flexible enough to ignore the numerous distractions and practice quiet listening too. A little practice is all we need.

Eric Butterworth wrote, "The key to healing, to the balanced life, may very well be in the cultivation of the 'fertile void' of the depths within."[4] The same listening the ancients required for survival, we require for a different kind of survival. Our sanity and our strength demand the cultivation of that fertile void of the depths within. Fortunately, we can build a consciousness of stillness. We can listen with a quiet mind.

The theme of quiet listening is heard often in the scriptures. In Habakkuk (2:20) we read, "The lord is in his holy temple; let all the earth keep silence before him." Elijah sought the presence of God. He found nothing in the wind, the earthquake, nor the fire. "And after the fire a still small voice." (I Kings 19:12) In the silence, made more profound after phonic events, was the presence of God. "In returning and rest shall ye be saved; in quietness and in confidence shall be your strength . . . And thine ears shall hear a word behind thee, saying this is the way, walk ye in it . . ." (Isaiah 30:15, 21) Be still; be still, be still. Listen for the voice of silence.

We search for the Kingdom of Heaven everywhere except where we are told that it is—*within us.* Listening to silence, we experience that inner realm of God's presence. Such times of silence provide cushions of quiet that act as shock absorbers for the thunderstorms of life. We seek the center of the whirling wheel and find a kingdom of peace. Herein is our quiet mind which ticks at its own delicious tempo.

You have already learned that the clamor and confusion are all in your own head. Even when you have evidence that the cacophony is in your milieu, you know that you, yourself, create and sustain the muddle. Think: STOP. Let it go; relax. Think less of more; work more on less. Put on the brakes. Use your command of "Whoa" to the runaway horses of your mind. The responsibility is your own. Stop!

As you have already seen, there are many ways and means of stopping. You can say to yourself, "Stop!"

and then start a new creative direction of thinking and living. You can enclose your prayers in silent stops that invite a bigger experience of the presence and power of God. Yet there is an additional type of stop—a way of praying while being "other" than praying. This is meditation. It begins by being alone and becoming quiet. This "stop" is your greatest "start."

Pascal said profoundly, "I have discovered that all human evil comes from this, man's being unable to sit still in a room."[5] How utterly simple! Find aloneness in nature or in a room by yourself. Plan for solitude. Set aside time to be quiet and alone.

"Actually these are among the most important times in one's life—when one is alone," writes Anne Morrow Lindbergh. "Certain springs are tapped only when we are alone."[6] However, we cannot live our lives totally in such aloneness. Most of us would not thrive on hermithood.

"The solution for me, surely, is neither in total renunciation of the world, nor in total acceptance of it," she says. "I must find a balance somewhere, or an alternating rhythm between these two extremes; a swinging of the pendulum between solitude and communion, between retreat and return."[7]

Our planning can create periodic cushions of quiet to buffer our activities. We need only to "come ye yourself apart . . . and rest a while." (Mark 6:31) We can swing the pendulum in an alternating rhythm between solitude and social intercourse. Such a time could be a quiet weekend on occasion. Perhaps an entire week of quiet could be arranged. Longer periods of time might be delicious yet impractical. Easiest to arrange are quiet spaces within every day.

No time to be alone? Nonsense! There are 1,440 minutes in every day. Roughly, two-thirds of that time is taken up in sleep and occupational responsibilities. That leaves eight hours, or 480 minutes, of which to use some part in solitude. A detour on your way to work can give you fifteen of those minutes in an aloneness where neither family nor work can intrude. Getting up earlier or awaking in the middle of the night can give you some valuable time alone.

Sometimes, the only room in the house where you are certain of privacy is the bathroom. Go in and close the door! Lock it! That can be your time to be truly alone and quiet. You are in your own head. Stop looking for reasons why you cannot be alone, and look for ways you can be. You can find a few of those 480 loose minutes to be by yourself.

If you should tell your friends that you cannot attend a social function because it conflicts with your time alone, you would be considered rude. "What commentary on our civilization, when being alone is considered suspect; when one has to apologize for it, make excuses, hide the fact that one practices it—like a secret vice!"[8] An appointment with the dentist is considered important; one with yourself should be thought equally important.

"Whoso would be a man, must be a nonconformist," said Emerson in his essay on Self-Reliance.[9] Perhaps you will need to "step to the music of a different drummer"[10] to dare to plan time for yourself. If the people in your life do not understand or respect the need to be alone, then you will need to run the risk of being considered "different." Remember Robert Frost's retort when questioned about his solitary walks. You too could reply, "Gnaw bark!" and find your detractors leaving you alone.

Actually, you do not need to be so specific. To say, "I am busy at that time," or "I have other plans that conflict with that event," is quite enough. When you accept an invitation, "yes" is answer enough and doesn't need to be qualified. Learn to think of "no" as equally valid an answer in itself. No protracted justification is necessary. "No" is a word and can be used. The more it is practiced the easier it becomes. You do not "need" to keep pace with your companions, especially when your time is taken for silent listening to the sacred sound of a different drummer. Plan your silent time and let nothing interfere.

Being alone is certainly not an end in itself, but a way to season the rest of life. Solitude is the salt of personhood.[11] It brings out the authentic flavor of every experience. Quietness is a joy to enhance all other joys. Giving to others is most enjoyable when balanced by being in touch with the fertile void. Experiencing God within the self creates a flavor to enrich everything else that is done. The need is to draw down to a new level of listening.

Have you ever awakened from sleep and realized you were unaware you were going to sleep or that you had slept at all until you experienced awakening? It is a common experience. Maybe it was a short nap, but you had no intention of sleeping and only after the fact were you aware of it. Meditation is often the same kind of experience. You are aware you have meditated only as you return to outer consciousness. You fulfill the requirements of outer and inner quiet. Your mental posture is one of listening. Then you become aware that you have touched something you had never touched before. Meditation has, of itself, occurred.

In deep meditation, the mind becomes "blank." On other levels of thought, you cannot make the mind blank—you are always thinking of something. When trying to think of nothing, you are only thinking about "thinking about nothing." However, in this deeper dimension of mind you listen in the silence and experience what Walter Starcke calls "the dying to the mind."[12] Draw down to this deeper level of listening and you are into deep silence of meditation. Here you experience what the mystics call "pure bliss" and "pure consciousness."

Intellectually, you cannot create this ultimate of meditation. It comes through the intuitive side of your being. You can, however, *invite* this healing, strengthening activity. Let your consciousness go as far as it will in quiet listening; then, release it further. Pluck the string of silence and gently hold yourself open. In the larger sense of living, such meditation is not an end in itself. Yet to experience such a greater depth of being, you must consider it as an end in itself. You want no other purpose but to hear the silence of God. "Therefore let your visit to that temple invisible be for naught but ecstasy and sweet communion . . . It is enough that you enter the temple invisible."[13] Usually you will know it has happened only "after the fact," when you "awaken."

By creating the conditions of inner and outer silence, and maintaining the disciplines that invite a listening-to-the-silence, you have placed your mind in a receptive posture. That is enough. There are benefits of peace and strength and health from simply opening your consciousness to *allow* a deeper meditation to occur. Do not be concerned if nothing happens. Your concern itself will be your major block.

Emerson stated the conditions of deeper meditation this way: "Place yourself in the middle of the stream of power and wisdom which animates all whom it floats, and you are without effort impelled to truth, to right, and a perfect contentment."[14] Think: STOP! Think a deeper Stop! Listen to the sound of silence. This is your greatest *Start-Think!*

When your mind becomes "blank" in this way, it is deeply full—profoundly quiet. In *The Spell of the Yukon,* Robert Service captures this inner hush:

> I've stood in some mighty-mouthed hollow
>   That's plumb full of hush to the brim;
> I've watched the big, husky sun wallow
>   In crimson and gold, and grow dim,
> Till the moon set the pearly peaks gleaming,
>   And the stars tumbled out, neck and crop;
> And I thought that I surely was dreaming,
>   With the peace of the world piled on top.[15]

Anyone who has been alone in nature knows what Service is talking about. The hills are alive with the sound of silence. Go alone, be still, and listen. The attitude of mind that is meditation is one of listening. Daily, observe minute pauses to balance your activities. As pausologists study the silence in speech, study the silence in your life. Regularly listen in silence.

There are many techniques today to draw you down to this deeper level of silence called meditation. You can practice disciplines ranging from ancient meditation rituals to modern space-age electronics. Don't confuse the method with the experience. Just as "the word is not the thing,"[16] neither is the method the experience. All that matters is that you open yourself to the possibility of greater silence.

You see, whether you chant a mantra, do breathing exercises, imagine quieting visions, attach electrodes to your head and monitor the feedback, sound affirmations slowly and listen after each one, or walk in some mighty-mouthed hollow, you are practicing deeper listening. Beyond the discipline of a technique is your letting go. "In quietness and in confidence shall be your strength." Enter the heart of silence, the heart cave, listen and be still.

You can enrich your life by simply going alone and being quiet. Senator Alan Cranston (D-Calif.) said, "Too often you're thinking what's thrust upon you by other people instead of what's in your own mind. You can create your own priorities when you're alone. When you're not alone, events and people determine them. I never let too much time go by without having some time by myself. Even in a campaign, I insist on it. Without it, I start making mistakes."[17]

Find your aloneness where you can. Close yourself in a room. Stay in bed for a day and simply think. Actually be by yourself in nature—find a deserted park or beach. You might find your aloneness in the anonymity of a darkened movie theater or a crowded airplane flight. You will find it!

Your life must be filled with silence, punctuated with spaces. Use many or few techniques to quiet your mind and body so that you can learn to listen to the sound of silence. Silence is *within* you; you can plan it to be *around* you as well. It is simple. Remember, ". . . that all human evil comes from this, man's being unable to sit still in a room."

Sit down and be still. Close your eyes and close your mouth. Two or three times a day, listen with a silent heart. At least once a day, build a consciousness of "hush." Make appointments with yourself for daily times and longer swings of the pendulum. Practice creating time to be alone and quiet.

You can be plumb full of hush to the brim! Add some of Walden Pond to your daily life. Season your personhood with the salt of solitude. *Stop-Think!* Think a deeper stop! *Start-Think!* Place yourself in the middle of that stream of quietness. Listening for the sound of silence creates a wonderfully new you. Every day you are newly born and newly alive. Listen to the silence. Listen to the hush. Listen.

CHAPTER FIFTEEN

Is There Life After *Birth*?

Eternal Life Is Today

"What happens to the enlightened man when he dies?" asked the student of his enlightened master-teacher.

The master replied, "Why ask me?"

"Because you are a Zen Master."

"Yes," said the master, "but not a dead Zen Master."[1]

Like the wise teacher, we do not know. We wonder, don't we! What does lie beyond? There are many theories: a place in the sky; an invisible dimension here on earth; the transmigration of souls back and forth into animals; reincarnation by being born into continuing human bodies. There is no proof for any of the beliefs. Whatever you believe must be accepted on faith. It is a matter of intuition, personal to each of us.

When "proof" is given, it is always subjective. Perhaps we will know some day; then again, perhaps we won't ever know. Actually, I wonder if we need to know. When we start asking questions about "life after death," we are searching for deeper meanings to life. That is enough! To face death is to question the purpose of

147

existence. What answers we find are not nearly as important as the questions we ask. Just to question the meaning of life is truly important.

An ancient wise man lamented, "Mankind is asleep. Must he die before he wakes?"[2] Hopefully, your answer would be "No." However, confronting death can be an awakening to life. If you knew you had only a week to live, you might well change your life-style. The things that were disturbing you would suddenly seem unimportant. Other things, perhaps neglected, could suddenly seem beautiful and important.

A friend of mine was driving home late at night. He had been detained at his work longer than he wanted to be; his day had been tedious, it was raining, and he was generally cross with the world. He could see the lights of a truck approaching in the opposite direction; all of a sudden, another set of lights was passing the truck! A car was in his lane heading straight for him. He swerved just in time to miss the oncoming car but landed with a jolt in the ditch. Both the truck and the other car continued without stopping.

My friend was not hurt and his car was not damaged. He sat there for some time—until his heart began to beat normally again. He said he experienced many emotions—fear, anger, relief—and he cried. All the worries of his day didn't matter any more. He thought of his wife; he thought of his children. He recalled the picnic they shared last week. He thought of many things, and he cried. Even the rainy night looked beautiful. A near-brush with death had caused a new awakening to life. From what he told me, a major change took place in him that night that continued for a long time.

Do not wait for a crisis to begin enjoying life. Start today. Even a close call with the end of this existence isn't necessary to begin to wake up. Ask the eternal questions: Where do we come from? Where are we going? What lies beyond the known? *Is there life after death?*

As you confront the conclusion of existence, your perspective about existence itself is changed. Suddenly it becomes important to ask, "What is life now?" "How alive are you now?" A new question automatically emerges from the previous ones: *"Is there life after BIRTH?"*

Life before or after this experience is an academic pursuit. What really counts is what your life is today. Are you really alive since you were born? Many of my friends believe in the theory of reincarnation—not the transmigration of souls into animal form, but successive life-times as human beings. If you are one who also believes in reincarnation, this is the life you have been "dying to get into." *Stop-Think-Start!* This is your heaven or hell, depending on what is going on in your head. How alive are you? *Is there life after birth?* Even though you cannot know all about the past or the future, you can know about today. What about it?

When a person looks closely at himself and his experience in life, he knows he will at some time leave his body. Yet, he knows he is more than a body and that "the real of him" must continue. Faith offers a certainty of life beyond that which we see today. By confronting the fragile fleetingness of life, we can experience an emerging faith in eternal life. Life is forever! There is continuity! The power of God-within cannot be limited to a particular body at a particular time.

Such a faith goes beyond the end and comes back upon

itself. Faith enlarges to embrace the integrity of every day—not only those beyond our physical lives, but including our existence here and now. Our faith convinces us that we live in God eternally. God will be with us in the life beyond that we cannot now see. Right now is our eternity in God.

"Man is born to live and not to prepare to live."[3] Life-eternal begins now. Live today! Start seeing God in all people and places. See with new eyes. Every day can be a *"reprieve"*—a golden gift of more joy and greater beauty. Awaken. Look at your life as it is now with new eyes. See the world around you as if you were seeing it for the first time. You were born to live now, so live with a new zest and a new intensity—a reprieve.

This concept of a reprieve was clearly experienced by Arthur Rubenstein, the concert pianist. Looking back, he realizes what a pitiable thing it was to try to take his own life many years ago:

> When I went out into the street, I came back from death. I was reborn. I suddenly realized what a damn fool I had made of myself. There were people moving through the streets, dogs were running around, flowers were growing in a little park—it was a wonderful, divine show. I learned then that happiness is not smiling or having money or being in good health, although these are conditions worth having. Happiness really is only living, taking life on its own terms.
>
> I'm passionately involved in life; I love its change, its color, its movement. To be alive, to be able to speak, to see, to walk, to have houses, music, paintings—it's all a miracle. I have adopted the technique of living life from miracle to miracle . . . [4]

Life is a miracle every day, if you are awake to it. "Only that day dawns to which we are awake," said Thoreau.[5] Awaken to life. Awaken to the dawn. Confront the eternal questions of life-after-death and see that the wonder of life is now, after birth, too. If reincarnation is true, then today is also life-after-death. The real point is this: today is eternal life; enjoy it now!

Eric Berne said, "The aware person is alive because he knows how he feels, where he is and when it is. He knows that after he dies the trees will still be there, but he will not be there to look at them again, so he wants to see them now with as much poignancy as possible."[6] To think should give a person a vitality—a greater aliveness. To *Stop-Think-Start!* should make us more aware, more alert, more alive.

You were born to live—to live now! "The aim of life is to be fully born, though its tragedy is that most of us die before we are thus born . . . The answer is . . . to develop one's awareness, one's reason, one's capacity to love, to such a point that one transcends one's own egocentric involvement and arrives at a new harmony and a new wonder with the world."[7] Jesus said so clearly, "I have come that men may have life in all its fullness." (John 10:10) Awaken to life today. Become fully born now!

Jesus spoke of being born anew. Being born to the presence of God, we see the wind-like fleetingness of life and embrace it. As we are awakened to God's presence in our silence, we are awakened to His activity in our living. An inner depth of listening quickens us to a new awareness of God in every daily action. God is not separate from His universe. With Thoreau we see "Heaven is under our feet as well as over our heads."[8] Awaken! New awareness! New life! New birth!

Stop-Think-Start! Life is lived from the inside out— it is all in your head! Your own attitude will determine what life is for you. As you are grounded in all the parts of yourself, you are in tune with God within your own consciousness. Through the law of substitution you can control your thinking to make life the beautiful experience it was meant to be. Then, creating those beckoning categories of answers-you-need, your imagination and faith create out of organic reality more of the beauty of life. Beyond your thinking and planning is the supreme silence where you let God be God in you. The knowing of that inner presence spreads to fill your entire experience with more aliveness. Your ultimate objective is to be in tune with God in the absolute and in all His phases of expression. Touch God at as many points in your life as you can. Every common bush is afire with God if you will only see! Wake up! Live now!

Every day can be a new dawn—a new beginning—a new birth. Every day you can set your mind to see the beauties all around you. When you see people and places around you with the vision of a reprieve, beauty can touch you so deeply that lesser feelings dissolve. Beauty, itself, can jolt you into rebirth. Every rock has its beauty. Any tree has its poetry to share. Each flower is its own miracle. Every person has something special to share. Awaken!

When you open your eyes after a meditation, look with renewed interest at your surroundings. Carry your meditation into every event. During the course of the day, practice seeing beauty—seeing God. Those lights trailing in the distance are like diamonds. That pattern of light and shadows is a ballet for you alone. The raindrops are creating a symphony; listen! The sky is beaded with stars in intricate patterns; look and see! How many colors are there in that hillside, that tree, that one leaf? Truly, ". . . to be awake is to be alive."[9] Such aliveness is yours now.

Thoreau practically sings, "If the day and the night are such that you greet them with joy, and life emits a fragrance like flowers and sweet-scented herbs, that is your success. The true harvest of my daily life is somewhat as intangible and indiscernible as the tints of morning or evening. It is a little stardust caught, a segment of the rainbow which I have clutched."[10] You must be born every day! While your physical birth may or may not have much life, this inner birth IS LIFE. Daily you are reborn to the divinity within yourself and the divinity of all things.

This is the life you have been waiting for! Don't delay any longer; the joy is within you. "The kingdom of God cometh not with observation: Neither shall they say, Lo here! or, lo there! for, behold, the kingdom of God is within you." (Luke 17:20-21) It's all in your head. *Stop-Think-Start!* Life can be beautiful if you look for that beauty. The suffering and the muddle are all within you too. What will it be? In the words of Milton, "The mind is its own place, and in itself can make a heav'n of hell, a hell of heaven."[11] It's up to you.

Every day is a reprieve—a fresh start. Practice looking for the wonder of life until it becomes a daily habit. You do not need to die before you awaken. Your every prayer, followed with silence, prepares you for birth. Every moment is the breath of God floating on the wind. Look and see! Eternal life is today! Awaken!

In the play *Our Town,* the young woman Emily has died and is permitted to return to Grover's Corners for one day. She is told it must be a quite ordinary day and she chooses her twelfth birthday. We see her in the kitchen at daybreak, watching her mother get breakfast. In the scene Emily is, at the same time, a child of twelve and a mature woman who can look back on life with the eyes of one who has left it. When she speaks as the child, her mother hears her, but when she speaks as the woman returned from the grave only the audience and the Stage Manager can hear. It goes like this:

Emily says softly, more in wonder than in grief, "I can't bear it. They're so young and beautiful. Why do they get old? I can't look at everything hard enough . . . Oh, Mama, just look at me one minute as though you really saw me . . . It goes so fast. We don't have time to look at one another."

She breaks down and sobs to the Stage Manager, "I didn't realize. So all this has been going on and we never noticed. Take me back—up the hill—to my grave. But first: Wait! One more look. Goodbye, goodbye, world. Goodbye, Grover's Corners . . . Mama and Papa . . . Goodbye to clock's ticking . . . and Mama's sunflowers and food and coffee. And new-ironed dresses and hot baths . . . and sleeping and waking up. Oh, earth, you are too wonderful for anyone to realize you."

Then she asks abruptly, "Does any human being ever realize life while they live it?—Every, every minute?"[12]

Eternal life is right now! Realize life while you live it! *Stop-Think-Start!*

The choice is yours—you can shape your own experience; you can stop any unwanted thought and really start to think. Accept your wonderful self; through the creative law of substitution, envision a new world of joy. Your awareness of the divinity within invites you to experience the wonder of life all around you.

The hardest thing is the most rewarding. *Stop-Think-Start!* Life is beautiful already. It's all in your head. *Stop-Think-Start!*

NOTES

INTRODUCTION

1. Thomas Carlyle, *Sartor Resartus* (New York: P. F. Collier & Son, MCMI), p. 144.
2. Ralph Waldo Emerson, "Intellect," in *Ralph Waldo Emerson: Essays and Journals* (Garden City, New York: Doubleday & Co., 1968), Lewis Mumford, ed., p. 226.

1. LIFE CAN BE BEAUTIFUL

1. Baba Ram Dass, *Be Here Now* (San Cristobal, New Mexico: Lama Foundation, 1972), Seventh Edition, Distributed by Crown Publishing Co., p. 33.
2. Robert Orben, *Cappers Weekly,* quoted in *The Reader's Digest* (July 1963), p. 84.
3. Earl Nightingale, "How's The World Treating You?" in *This is Earl Nightingale* (Garden City, New York: Ferguson and Doubleday Companies, 1969), p. 46.
4. Earl Wilson, Publishers-Hall Syndicate.
5. *Capper's Weekly,* no additional information available.
6. Lloyd Shearer, "Sophia Loren—Woman of La Mancha." *Parade* (May 14, 1972), pp. 4–7.
7. Konrad Adenauer, "Quotable Quotes," *The Reader's Digest* (No date available), p. 194.
8. *Bits & Pieces* (Fairfield, New Jersey: The Economic Press, item undated), Marvin Gregory, ed., pp. 22–23.

9. Erich Brandeis, King Features Syndicated Column appeared in 400 newspapers, *Citizen-News,* Hollywood (January 30, 1951), Article photographically reproduced in Harry Owens, *Sweet Leilani.*

2. MISERY IS OPTIONAL

1. Ralph Waldo Emerson, "Prudence," *op. cit.,* p. 181.
2. Ella Wheller Wilcox, "You and To-Day," from *1000 Quotable Poems* (New York: Harper and Bro., 1937), Thomas Curtis Clark, ed.

3. WHY DO THINGS GET IN A MUDDLE?

1. Gregory Bateson, *Steps To An Ecology of Mind* (New York: Ballantine Books, 1972), pp. 3-8. This collection of Dr. Bateson's writings is a vastly stimulating book.
2. *Ibid.* This example is an adaptation of one of Bateson's in his metalogue.
3. Marcus Aurelius Antonius, "Meditations, IV," in John Bartlett, *Familiar Quotations* (Boston: Little, Brown and Co., 1968), fourteenth edition, p. 141.
4. Alfred Adler, *Understanding Human Nature* (New York: Greenberg, 1927), Walter Beran Wolfe, translator, p. 255.
5. Nena O'Neill and George O'Neill, *Shifting Gears* (New York: Avon Books, 1975), p. 140.
6. Alan Lakein, *How to Get Control of Your Time and Your Life* (New York: Signet Books, 1974), pp. 28-29. Mr. Lakein is a renowned time-management consultant. His book is excellent.
7. Alexander Solzhenitsyn, *One Day In the Life of Ivan Denisovich* (New York: E. P. Dutton, 1963), p. 158.
8. James Allen, *As A Man Thinketh* (Mt. Vernon, New York: The Peter Pauper Press), pp. 25-27.

4. LOOK BEFORE YOU LEAP

1. Lewis Carroll, "Alice's Adventures in Wonderland," in *The Complete Works of Lewis Carroll* (London: the Nonesuch Press, 1939), p. 80.
2. Dr. Herbert Benoit, The Supeme Doctrine (New York: Pantheon Books, 1955) quoted in Vernon Howard, *The Mystic Path To Cosmic Power* (New York: The Paperback Library, 1969), p. 95.
3. Frederick S. Perls, *Gestalt Therapy Verbatim* (Lafayette, Calif.: Real People Press, 1969), John Stevens, ed., p. 40.

5. BEYOND YOUR HAT AND YOUR BOOTS

1. William Shakespeare, *Hamlet, Prince of Denmark,* Act III, Scene 1.
2. Edward Stanford Martin, "Mixed," quoted in Everett L. Shostrom, *Man, the Manipulator* (New York: Bantam Books, 1968), p. 74.
3. Walt Whitman, "Song of Myself," in *The Complete Poetry and Prose of Walt Whitman* (New York: Pellegrini & Cudahy, 1948), Vol. I, stanza 51, p. 113.
4. Charles Fillmore, *Keep a True Lent* (Lee's Summit, Mo.: Unity School of Christianity, 1957), p. 110.
5. Leo Tolstoy, quoted in Everett L. Shostrom, *Man, the Manipulator* (New York: Bantam Books, 1968), p. 61.
6. Marcus Aurelius Antonius, quoted in Joshua Loth Liebman, *Peace of Mind* (New York: Simon & Schuster, 1947), p. 6.
7. Rollo May, *The Art of Counseling* (New York: Abingdon Press, 1967), p. 177.
8. Ralph Waldo Emerson, quoted in Liebman, *op.cit.,* p. 37.
9. Oliver Cromwell, quoted in John Bartlett, *Familiar Quotations, op. cit.,* p. 328. The exact text is: "Mr. Levy, I

desire you would use all your skill to paint my picture truly like me, and not flatter me at all; but remark all these roughnesses, pimples, warts, and everything as you see me, otherwise I will never pay a farthing for it."

10. Carl Jung, *Modern Man in Search of a Soul* (New York: Harcourt, Brace & Co., 1933) W. S. Dell & C. F. Baynes, translators, p. 235.

11. Dr. Irene Kassorla, *Putting It All Together* (New York: Hawthorne Books, 1973), p. 202.

12. Roberto Assagioli, "The Dance of the Many Selves," Synthesis (Vol. 1, Number 1, 1974), p. wb56.

6. TAKE OFF YOUR SHOES

1. Paul Tillich, *The Shaking of the Foundations* (New York: Charles Scribner's Sons, 1948), p. 57.

2. Elizabeth Barrett Browning, "Aurora Leigh," bk VII, 1. 820.

3. H. Emily Cady, *Lessons in Truth* (Lee's Summit, Mo.: Unity School of Christianity, 1955), p. 15.

7. DISPLACE; REPLACE; SUBSTITUTE

1. Charles Darwin, "The Descent of Man," ch. 4, quoted in Bartlett, *op. cit.,* p. 628.

2. Johnny Mercer wrote the music and Harold Arlen wrote the words for this popular W. W. II song.

3. Emmet Fox, quoted in Ernest Wilson, *Soul Power* (Lee's Summit, Mo.: Unity School of Christianity, 1963), p. 35.

4. Judge Thomas Troward, quoted in Charles Roth, "Breaking the Spell," *Weekly Unity* (August 8, 1967), pp. 1–2.

5. William and Ellen Hartley, "Phobias: Coping with Irrational Fears," *Science Digest* (September 1974), pp. 63–68.

A report on work by Dr. Wallace W. Wilkins at the University of Miami.
6. Eric Butterworth, "What are You Saying to Yourself?" *Challenge* (June 1972).
7. Dr. David Knox, *Marriage, Happiness, a Behavorial Approach to Counseling* (at this writing, further information unavailable).
8. H. Emily Cady, *op. cit.,* p. 33.

8. TALK UP TO YOURSELF

1. *Good Business Magazine,* former publication of Unity School of Christianity, Lee's Summit, Mo., (July 1962), p. 3.
2. Blaise Pascal, quoted in William D. Ellis, "Try Talking to Yourself," *The Reader's Digest,* (July 1971), p. 135.
3. Lewis Carroll, "Through the Looking Glass," in *The Complete Works, op. cit.,* p. 184.
4. I have no idea where this line originated, but what a good one it is!
5. Emerson, "History," *op. cit.,* p. 79.
6. Dr. Bernard Berkowitz and Mildred Newman with Jean Owen, *How to be Your Own Best Friend* (New York: Random House, 1971), p. 45.
7. *Ibid.,* pp. 50–51.
8. Emerson, "Spiritual Laws," *op. cit.,* p. 146.
9. William D. Ellis, "Try Talking to Yourself," *The Reader's Digest* (July 1971), p. 135.
10. Jhan and June Robbins, "You Don't Know Your Own Strength," *This Week Magazine,* (December 4, 1960), p. 16.
11. Thomas Troward, *The Edinburgh Lectures* (New York: Dodd, Mead and Co., 1909), p. 54.

9. ACT IN COLD BLOOD

1. Bill Vaughn in the *Kansas City Star*.
2. Johann W. Goethe, quoted in Gene Emmet Clark, *Let's Talk About You* (Santa Monica, Calif.: Creative Life Foundation), p. 15.
3. Carlyle, *Sartor Resartus, op. cit.,* p. 148.
4. Emerson, "Compensation," *op. cit.,* p. 123.
5. Henry David Thoreau, quoted in *Light From Many Lamps* (Simon Schuster: New york, 1951), Lillian Eichler Watson, ed., p. 235.
6. Ad for recruits for U. S. Navy, appeared in *Newsweek*.
7. Friedrich Wilhelm Nietzsche, (1844–1900) no source located.
8. Charles W. Cole, "Find New Meanings," *This Week Magazine* (March 30, 1960), p. 2.
9. From *Monopoly,* game by Parker Bros.
10. William D. Ellis, "Your Echo Effect," *The Rotarian* (August 1973).
11. William James, *The Principles of Psychology* (New York: Dover Publishing, Inc., 1950), p. 321.
12. *Ibid.,* p. 450.

10. THE OPEN INVITATION

1. Lao-Tzu, *Tao Te Ching* (New York: Vintage Books by Random House, 1972), FOUR.
2. William Blake quoted in Joseph C. Pearce, *The Crack in the Cosmic Egg* (New York: Pocket Books, 1974), p. 47.
3. Joseph Chilton Pearce, *The Crack in the Cosmic Egg* (New York: Pocket Books, 1974). I am indebted to Mr. Pearce for many of the concepts used in this chapter and in my life.
4. *Ibid.,* p. 7.
5. Andrew Weil, *The Natural Mind,* exerpted in *Psychology Today* (October 1972), p. 62.

6. D. D. Kosambi, "Living Prehistory in India," *Scientific American,* quoted in Joseph Pearce, *op. cit.,* p. 109.
7. Fillmore, *Keep a True Lent, op. cit.,* p. 65.
8. Leonard Feinberg, "Fire Walking in Ceylon," *The Atlantic Monthly* (March 1959), quoted in Joseph Pearce, *op. cit.,* p. 104.
9. Gilbert M. Grosvenor & Donna Grosvenor, "Ceylon," *The National Geographic Magazine* (April 1966), Vol. 129, no. 4, p. 485. Also quoted in Pearce, *op. cit.,* p. 107, but I was able to locate the original magazine and read the article in its entirety.
10. Pearce, *op. cit.,* p. 112.
11. *Ibid.,* p. 5.
12. *Ibid.,* p. 113 (not a direct quote).
13. I John 3:2.

11. HEALTH: A PROCESS OF IDENTIFICATION

1. William S. Porter, "The Last Leaf," in *The Complete Works of O. Henry* (Garden City, New York: Garden City Publ. Co., 1937), pp. 1414–1419.
2. Plato, *The Republic.*
3. Dr. Henry Huber, M.D., Attending Surgeon, French Hospital, New York, "The Importance of 'The Will to Live,' " *This Week* (Apr 15, 1962).
4. Dr. Arnold A. Hutschnecker, M. D., *The Will to Live* (New York: Cornerstone Library, 1966), p. 34.
5. Howard R. & Martha E. Lewis, *Psychosomatics* (New York: The Viking Press, 1972).
6. Dr. O. Carl Simonton, M. D., "The Role of Emotions in the Development and Treatment of Cancer," the Fillmore Lectures, Seattle, WA., March 7, 1975, from my lecture notes of his address. Dr. Simonton is a radiologist in Fort Hood, Texas, who has been using meditation with other treatments for cancer since 1971.

7. Dr. Ian Stevenson, "Psychomatic Medicine," Part I, *Harper's* (July 1954).
8. Dr. William Menninger, *Newsweek* (December 1958).
9. Fillmore, *Keep a True Lent, op. cit.,* pp. 38–39.
10. Eric Butterworth, *Unity of All Life* (New York: Harper & Row, 1969), p. 78.
11. Edmund Sinnott, *Matter, Mind, and Man,* quoted in Eric Butterworth, *Ibid.,* p. 80.
12. Dr. Elmer Green, my lecture notes of his presentation on biofeedback and mind control, Fillmore Lectures, Seattle, WA., March 7, 1975. Dr. Green is head of the Psychophysiology Lab doing research at the Menninger Foundation in Topeka, Kansas.
13. Dr. Robert H. Schuller, *Enjoy Emotional Health, Wholeness and Happiness* (Garden Grove, Calif.: Hour of Power, 1972), p. 8.
14. Charles Fillmore, attributed to him although no direct quote or reference was located.
15. Butterworth, *op. cit.,* p. 81.
16. Lennart Nilsson, *Behold Man* (Time-Life Book). Photo reprinted in *Science Digest* (November 1974).

12. DON'T THINK ABOUT HIPPOPOTAMUS

1. Walter B. Pitkin, *The Art of Learning,* quoted in Janet Newton Batchler, "Don't Think About Hippopotamus," *Good Business* (January 1962), p. 37.
2. Patricia Ellen Ricci, poster (Chicago, Ill.: Argus Communications, 1970), poster no. 272.
3. Emmet Fox, *The Golden Key,* (Unity Village, Mo.: Unity School of Christianity, 1973), Special Unity Edition, p. 5.
4. Charles Fillmore, *Jesus Christ Heals* (Lee's Summit, Mo.: Unity School of Christianity, 1955), p. 14.

13. AN ALTOGETHER OTHER DIMENSION

1. Emerson, "Spiritual Laws," *op. cit.,* p. 147.
2. Elizabeth Goudge, *Pilgrim's Inn* (New York: Coward-McCann, 1948), p. 60.
3. Charles Fillmore, *Christian Healing* (Lee's Summit, Mo.: Unity School of Christianity, 1964), p. 8.
4. Albert Einstein, "What I Believe," *Forum* (October 1930) p. 194. More specifically, he said, "It is enough for me to contemplate the mystery of conscious life perpetuating itself through all eternity, to reflect upon the marvelous structure of the universe . . . and to try humbly to comprehend even an infinitesimal part of the intelligence manifested in nature."
5. Emerson, "The Over-Soul," *op. cit.,* p. 209.
6. Walt Whitman, "When I Heard The Learn'd Astronomer," *The Complete Poetry and Prose of Walt Whitman* (New York: Pellegrini and Cudahy, 1948), Vol. I., p. 256.
7. Paul Brunton, *Discover Yourself* (New York: E. P. Dutton & Co., 1939) quoted in Vernon Howard, *The Mystic Path, op. cit.,* p. 91.
8. Daniel Yankelovich, as quoted in conversation by T. George Harris, "To Cope With Uncertainty," *Psychology Today* (November 1975), p. 4.
9. William James, *The Varieties of Religious Experience* (New York: Modern Library, 1929), p. 506.
10. Psalm 46:10, "Be still and know that I am God . . ."

14. THE SOUND OF SILENCE

1. "The Sounds of Silence," *Science Digest* (May 1973), pp. 30–31.
2. Emily Dickinson, *Emily Dickinson Poems* (Cleveland: Fine Editions Press, 1948), Mabel L. Todd and T. W. Higginson, editors, p. 195.

3. Kahlil Gibran, *Mirrors of the Soul* (New York: Philosophical Library, 1965) Joseph Sheban, translator, from the foreword.
4. Eric Butterworth, "Escape To The Center," *Unity Magazine* (April 1972), p. 21.
5. Blaise Pascal, Bartlett, *op. cit.,* p. 363.
6. Anne Morrow Lindbergh, *Gift From The Sea* (New York: Pantheon Books, 1955), p. 50.
7. *Ibid.,* p. 30.
8. *Ibid.,* p. 50.
9. Emerson, "Self-Reliance," *op. cit.,* p. 92.
10. Henry David Thoreau, *Walden* (Columbus, Ohio: Charles E. Merrill Co., 1969), p. 348.
11. This well-turned phrase doesn't sound original with me but I have no idea where it came from.
12. Walter Starcke, *The Ultimate Revolution* (New York: Harper & Row, 1969), p. 123.
13. Kahlil Gibran, *The Prophet* (New York: Alfred A. Knopf, 1972), p. 75.
14. Emerson, "Spiritual Laws," *op. cit.,* p. 134.
15. Robert Service, "The Spell of the Yukon," probably published by Barse and Hoplins, New York, as were many of his other works, before 1921.
16. S. I. Hayakawa, *Language In Action* (New York: Harcourt, Brace & Co., 1941).
17. Alan Cranston, quoted in Marlene Simons, "Solitude: Alone But Not Lonely," Los Angeles Times Service in *Honolulu Star Bulletin-Advertiser* (November 18, 1973).

15. IS THERE LIFE AFTER *BIRTH*?

1. Rollo May, discussion following lecture for Association of Humanistic Psycholopgy, Honolulu, Hawaii, (Summer, 1973).
2. Believed from the *Koran.*

3. Boris Pasternak, (1890–1960), no source located.
4. Arthur Rubenstein, *Time Magazine* (February 25, 1966), Cover story, p. 88.
5. Thoreau, *op. cit.,* p. 357.
6. Eric Berne, *Games People Play* (New York: Grove Press, 1964), p. 180.
7. D. T. Suzuki, Eric Fromm, and Richard DeMartino, *Zen Buddhism and Psychoanalysis* (New York: Harper & Row, 1960), pp. 87–88.
8. Thoreau, *op. cit.,* p. 304.
9. *Ibid,* p. 98.
10. *Ibid,* p. 233.
11. John Milton, "Paradise Lost," in *Literature in English* (New York: Henry Holt Co., 1949), lines 254 & 255.
12. Thornton Wilder, *Our Town* (New York: Harper & Row, 1957), pp. 97–100.